To Terry & Matthew

All my love

xxx

Visible Darkness

Super Storm Yolanda International Name Haiyan

by Emy Cajipe

DORRANCE
PUBLISHING CO
EST. 1920
PITTSBURGH, PENNSYLVANIA 15238

Dorrance Publishing Co
585 Alpha Drive
Suite 103
Pittsburgh, PA 15238
Visit our website at *www.dorrancebookstore.com*

ISBN: 978-1-4809-1261-8
eISBN: 978-1-4809-1583-1

Emy

As a six-year-old child in the late 1950s, my life started to turn into darkness during the wake of my father who I adored and loved so much. I told myself that he would wake up on time to prepare my food—my favorite, warm steamed rice mixed with condensed milk—debone my fish, take a walk, or swim after his long sleep in Uncle Simplicio's living room, surrounded by friends, relatives mourning his sudden death.

My life revolved around my father; it was just the two us. After nights of dreaming of my father coming home, I realized he would never ever come back to put me to bed. One night, I bolted upright out of a sound sleep and saw my father before me calling my name "Emy." It was the most compelling dream I ever experienced about my father, a message that woke me so strongly, it was as if he had spoken aloud: "Take care my child and good-bye." And a calm farewell instantly fell over my soul as he kissed me and was gone.

I was a sad confused little girl. I felt so alone even though love surrounded me. I saw the visible darkness of my life and only the deep humanity of the people, the beauty of the land, and kindness of my own people saved my loneliness and sanity and gave me whatever measure of joy I could take a hold then as a child.

In the afternoon, when there was no school, I roamed around Hinangutdan freely and walked alone, taking short cuts in between neighborhoods yards to visit my Uncle Tito and his wife, Aunt Elena, and my cousins. Their house was by the Hinangutdan seashore. There was a chair and plate waiting for me.

Poverty all around. No sewers or restrooms. The sandy streets followed along the pure white shoreline where houses were built on sticks above the waterline. A bamboo bridge extension to a little hut, enough for one person to squat, would be the outhouse to the open sea. As a child I would wander around aimlessly in and out of my relative's houses and dark little stores. One of my Uncle's family would take me in and they made a place for me a place to sit. They offered me company and food. Sometimes they would ask me to stay longer and we would cook my favorite purple sweet rice, a mixture of coconut milk, brown sugar, and anise seed. I was a family member to them and until now I cannot let go. I am always welcome. I learn from them just go on no matter what happens without complaint and get the job done. Ironically, it may be one of the lessons that encouraged me to start my SMC Educational Fund foundation.

During the two months before Haiyan arrived, I had been in the coastal community of Hinangutdan, Santa Rita, Samar, Philippines to help rebuild a local church (Uncle Simplicio had once donated it in his property) and set up educational programs for the island's impoverished youth as a social investment to the needy families while visiting some family members. To this day, being in Hinangutdan, even though the new generation does not know me, always soothes me.

Each time I would be home visiting my Uncle in Hinangutdan, Santa Rita, Samar, life had not changed—no electricity or phones. TVs in cities as Tacloban City, Leyte and to remote areas such as Hinangutdan, Santa Rita, Samar were a novelty, a few families received two TV channels that everyone would gather around. I saw children extending their necks like cranes to watch a TV show in their neighbor's window.

The social norm is so far apart I still faced a massive culture shock. I had been in Samar on the mission trip, a working vacation that meant most of my early morning coffee hours, I'd take the weight off my feet in the loggia at my family home in Hinangutdan, Santa Rita, Samar by the beach, watching the spellbinding waves and the immense satisfaction that can put forward.

The waves I am about to describe were the most atrocious in speed and violence that I have underwent, and yet beyond a definite point, I do not know how to put its aggression down, except by piling one adjective to another, so that in the end, I should put into terms no turn of phrase that is at all an excruciating overstatement.

It took me some time to take hold of the deep-seated rationale for this hopelessness around the traumatic experiences and nightmares. Furthermore, my story, the insurrection of which I myself lived through, gave me the feeling that I should write a compelling story that would describe the nightmare of the storm and remarkable path to survival.

Prior to my retirement in August 2013, I cashed in some of my 401k to fulfill my longtime dream to build a resource center in my hometown of Hinangutdan, Santa Rita, Samar, Philippines. My husband and I share the same passion and of helping the less fortunate. A few times a year we would send boxes of goods to families in my childhood town of Hinangutdan. We would send educational material, computers, clothing, slippers, food, musical instruments and uniforms for the Hinangutdan Elementary School Marching Drum and Percussion band.

In addition, we'd throw a Christmas party for street children in Catbalogan City the Island of Samar in the form of slippers, children's books for underprivileged children, and monetary awards for the graduating class of G. Tuazon High in Catbalogan. Every year, Tim and I will do our good deeds. I am touched, and my heart fills with happiness to see all the pictures of innocent and joyful faces of these children that Oscar Maribojoc provided me that I asked of him during the events.

September, 2013: A month before my visit to Samar. This time it would have more meaning than the previous visits, as I planned to visit family in Tacloban, Santa Rita, and Hinangutdan and work on my Uncle's donated church, which needed some touching up. Next to the church, my Uncle reserves a parcel of land under a deed in my name. It remains untouched, a piece of property where I use to run around carefree as a child. For the last forty years, I've visited every now and then. During this visit I have started to put up a fence to start the construction for a resource center, a cosmetology training center, for those interested in that field of which I am a professional.

In addition, there is a small community library. I have collected books in Rapid City, South Dakota, from a long time friend, Mrs. Ardie Crawford, and my *No Hat Society* friend that I briefly got to know, the late English professor, Josephine Mason Lee of South Dakota School of Mines, an honorable lady, who herself donated her body to science for educational purposes. Her lifetime book collection will be forever enjoyed in my family's own private foundation for my late Uncle Simplicio Mendez Cajipe, the SMC Educational Fund.

My uncle has been gone since 1992 at ninety-two years old. After my father, Tirso, passed away, he did his best to fill the shoes my father left behind. My meaningful visits were always fresh, and a gnawing grief is still in my heart after I left all those years ago. I wanted to set up an educational program for the impoverished youth of parts of Samar Island, visit the Samar State University in Catbalogan, where I wanted to send the qualified students for my program. I wanted to meet the school officials and tour the university.

This is a personal passion of mine that I inherited from my Uncle, who provided me with shelter, guidance, and love after my father's death. As I reflect back on my life, I feel blessed for everthing I have and all my life experiences, the good times and the bad, because they made me what I am today. I want to inspire people; for I believe everyone is capable of making a difference.

I do not earn a lot, but I want to give back what I can. Tim, my husband, Brian, Ian, and AJ, our children, are supportive of my passion to help some of the underprivileged children, and I always make my children be a part of this. Hopefully, some day, they will continue on this legacy. I have faith in each of us to do something good, to start with a handful of people and my family, one at a time.

My Uncle Simplicio provided teachings and opportunities to succeed and be good citizens to me and my cousins. He taught me the fortunate should help the less providential. He backed up his teachings by taking responsibility for Caloy a two-year-old orphan child and lone survivor of a capsized ferry. He cared for another abandoned child, Carol, for three more years before he passed away.

Uncle Simplicio and his wife, Cresencia, had staked out a claim on the shores of Hinangutdan, Santa Rita, Samar after WWII, traveling by boat from

Intramuros Manila, Philippines where the Japanese held them captive. Hectares of virgin land where he intended to plant abaca, coconuts and assorted fruit trees, mango, avocado, papaya, jackfruit, star apple, fruit of the gods, and wild guava trees. Each time I go for a walk around the property, I see a new guava seedling. Cocoa and coffee trees. Lemon trees and grapefruit.

It was a beautiful jungle of fruit trees, where nobody would ever go hungry. There was one Ylang Ylang tree that grew between our house and the church. When it was in full bloom it had beautiful white flowers dangling like earrings from the many branches. It was a huge tree and looked like a monument with the branches reaching toward the blue skies. It was beautiful. The entire community enjoyed the rejuvenating and relaxing scent.

At nights, when the moon was shining brightly, blue skies and the stars flickering, adding the beauty of the moon, I would just sit and watch the constellations that would appear to be really close to me. We would also be running around, playing hide-and-seek, or just sitting around telling stories. As a child, I saw the beautiful, full eclipse of the moon. It was unforgettable, a celebration of the traditional folklore. While the eclipse was happening, people started pounding the wooden mortar, and all pregnant women would be hiding inside or under the house to not get caught during the solar eclipse of the moon.

Moreover, on a rising slope of ground, overlooking the Canjabas Bay, Uncle Simplicio had built a traditional Filipino wooden house, a sprawling rectangle off the ground, sitting on giant wood pillars. A comfortable and unpretentious house in the middle of his land, it was roomy and away from neighbors. Hidden from the main street by wooden fences, the gate was actually a knee-high bench, always open, to a path that leads to four stairs and an open, sprawling veranda and a separate cottage for the bathroom.

Surrounded by bougainvillea, flowerpots of flowers collected by Aunt Cresencia on the ledges, and orchids hanging from the ceiling for privacy, another four steps lead to the main, front, double doors made of strong mahogany to the main house. The spacious veranda was used as a work area at times for weaving nipa and storing the copra that are ready for shipping to Tacloban and rice after drying, packed and ready for rice mill.

The roof was made of nipa, since he had an abundance of them on his land. There was a glass skylight and the walls were made of mahogany wood. A very vivid burgundy colored teak wood was used in the floors. Some of the walls had big picture windows. All kinds of tropical birds' melodious chirps could be heard in the early mornings and a special guest of a lone, huge, white owl would perch by my window at times as would my pet water buffalo rest his flared nostrils.

I remember many memories of my early days in Uncle Simplicio's home, it was bursting with life and high-quality times with big parties most of the time. On August 19, there was a yearly formal procedure for my birthday. I always looked forward to it. As a child, the teachers would announce no class on that day, and everyone would be invited to our house for my birthday. It was like a holiday—no school, and everyone in Hinangutdan was at our home for a huge party and roasted pigs. I was nobility, but Uncle Simplicio always had a simper on his face; little did I know it was President Manuel L. Quezon's birthday holiday that was the same date as mine.

A family member, relatives, or just friends would arrive from different parts of the province and might stay for weeks or months. During their stay the men would farm and fish while the women would feed the chickens and pigs, help prepare the food, and do other chores around the home. It seemed like someone was always visiting and knew just what needed to be done.

My childhood was full of life and laughter as I hung out with all of them. Once, a little chick was sick, the eyes full of gunk, and Aunt Cresencia told me to bury it alive. The chick was so heartbreaking that I hid the chick under a huge root of an old jackfruit tree and took care of the chick, bringing it back to life. Another incident: a pig was crying because its piglet's little tosh was halfway out. I couldn't stand listening to its cry, so I pulled the piglet out. Uncle Simplicio told me that I ought to be a doctor.

As a child, during high tides, the lagoon waters were beautiful, shimmering, clear, blue water so irresistible that you could not help but jump in. The water temperature was always perfect from the heat from the scorching sun. The waves as they rolled over the white sands would wash away my footprints almost as quickly I created them. The white sandy beach glittered from the sun, and on low tide it was endless. The two rocky points that make Hinangutdan look like a half moon were connected so that you could run across from one end to the other. Cousin Betty and I would go out to dig clams and oysters and look for other sea creatures in the tide pools.

I watched the anglers lay net traps (laya) at high tides, marked with a buoy after the nets had been laid. The anglers would punch the water for noise to draw the fish to their trap. At low tide, they used a net attached to two bamboo poles shaped like a V (sudsud) and pushed the net to the sandy beach to catch shrimp.

On the projection of Hinangutdan, mountain slopes seem to grow toward beautiful, clear powder blue skies and are covered with endless coconut trees. Most of the people are farmers and work at some coconut plantation belonging to the wealthy landowners, a relationship between the rich and the poor.

During the early morning before the eastern sunshine at low tides, a few steps away from our home, I would accompany my Great Grandmother Saturnina to the beach. She'd soak in the shallow area and clean her teeth with the fine, white sand from the beach. I would simply do the chore, playfully and gently gathering a thin film sack full of water attached to the sandy beach, put it in a bucket, and bring it home with us. Until her death, I never questioned what it was, and to this day of my adult years, it remains a mystery.

Once we got home my Great Grandmother would pour the thin film sack full of water in to a tub and add water she had already boiled with some leaves. She would soak in the tub to rinse away the salt water of the sea. It was our daily, early morning ritual, her beauty secret to live a long, healthy life, and she lived to 120 years old and had most of her teeth.

Typhoons are frequent in our province. The island people are aware of the damage that comes with a typhoon. The people are drawn to the water like coconuts; shanty homes along the beach are lost as waves rolled in and carry the shanty home to the open sea, and they build again. After Typhoon Haiyan, I learned that they want to live by the water because their livelihood is fishing. They are resilient people. Coconut trees uprooted, rice paddies and root crops flooded, but still they move on.

Super Typhoon Haiyan destroyed certain areas of the Visayas, and Hinangutdan was one of them. It will take years or decades to rebuild; the already neglected schools are left without roofs. The surging waters and high tides destroyed the fishponds in the Canjabas Bay. The bangus (the national fish) lived on brackish water, washed from the ponds to the shallow bay, and people waded into the bay to grab the fish before they die.

As a child, I actually looked forward to the days during the typhoon. While waiting for the typhoon to subside, Aunt Cresencia would make hot chocolate and coffee all day to keep warm. She also made purple sweet rice and would fry some dried fish. We sat around our long table eating as I was mixing hot chocolate with my coffee. It was so good, and everyone was enjoying my concoction—I did not realize I had discovered café mocha. We harvested our coffee and cacao for personal use, and some we gave away.

After the typhoon, my cousin Dondon and I would go to the church that was next to our house, collect the used candles, and run as fast as we could to the white sandy beach. We would see hundreds of crabs on the beach after the typhoon, walking around on the beach and we would catch some of them. Next we would light a candle and stick it on the crab's shell. The hot wax would drip on the back of the crab, and they run around like crazy. Another time after the typhoon, everything had been blown away to the ground, we collected the guavas on the ground, and Aunt Cresencia taught us how to make a guava jelly.

As the sun dried the debris left by typhoon, we had fun clearing and gathering the leaves and branches, putting them into mounds and setting them on fire, a chore that Uncle Simplicio would make look like a game for us while the birds chirped a melody above the almost shaved fruit trees. Our property never looked pretty after a typhoon. The trees looked so sad and made me sad, too. There was no pleasant solitude when everything around you was sad and pathetic looking.

I would spend more of my time riding my water buffalo up and down the hillside behind our house. I would lay on the grassy knoll in wonder as I watched the water buffalo roll around for a mud bath. He was the most pampered buffalo. He was not the working kind and he was my companion, my pet and loyal friend. My water buffalo was my slow motion horse. He'd stop and eat some grass and *moo* on as we surveyed the land.

It is amazing that after a few weeks, the surrounding area is happy again. The fruit trees start sprouting new branches and new leaves. I'd watch the new buds of flowers before I sleep and wake up in the morning to full blooms.

My Uncle Simplicio's love and compassion manifests within me, his teachings live on by doing good, choosing positive words and actions, things that were hard for me to understand in my young mind. Everyday enhances as I grow older.

At one time, Uncle Simplicio introduced me to a new friend inside a little cage made of bamboo on a bed of coconut husk. Uncle Simplicio warned me that this would be a short-lived relationship that would last days, "an actual learning experience that I will carry through life," he said. This new friend is fat and as it crawls, I see it has at least a dozen feet; it is about ten inches long and hairy. I am hesitant to touch it. It was a rare caterpillar and he asked me to watch and care for the caterpillar everyday and make notes as it changed, the osmosis and transformation of life, for it will teach me a beautiful lesson.

After days of nurturing the caterpillar, it matured into a butterfly. I held it gently in my hands and set it free out my bedroom window as I tearfully watched and said good-bye to my friend. The big, colorful wings span to eight inches each; it gracefully soars, noiselessly flapping its wings into thin air. An amazing humor, an anecdote, that I treasure all my life, a beautiful, colorful, giant butterfly. The butterfly was beautiful indeed.

After a year in Hinangutdan, my father, Tirso, passed away and left me under the care of Uncle Simplicio and Aunt Cresencia as their own daughter, for they were unable to have children of their own. My mother was alive but never came to claim me. I do not remember much of her, but I had a vivid memory of my father, Tirso. Uncle Simplicio kept a picture of my father in his U.S. Army Scout uniform, and I dreamt of him often.

My father, Tirso, was a boxer, and he was an entertainer for the U.S. Army while he was scouting for them against the Japanese. I believe that is where my three sons got some of their genes. Because of my Father's service with the United States Army as a US Scout, I earned funding to go to college when I was old enough.

Uncle Simplicio Cajipe was the defense lawyer for the town of Santa Rita, which was a few miles walk along the shoreline from our home in Hinangutdan. There was not a road at that time but a grassy path. We chose to walk to Santa Rita on the beach, which I cherished profoundly. The tree branches appeared to spread toward the sea, as if they were trying to reach the water.

The beauty of nature on this island impressed me at a young age. Hinangutdan is hidden away from Santa Rita by at least three rocky points and white sand beaches in between. As we emerged from the third rocky point I saw the long Santa Rita pier from the sandy beach of Binakalan. I never knew how long the trek was, but it was not tiresome for my little short legs.

Occasionally, Uncle Simplicio would allow me to sit inside the courtroom and watch him at work during a trial. He was a well-respected man and wanted to help people. He knew how poor the folks were, so he would accept any type of payment for his services. This might include live chickens or pigs, fish, fruits, or root crops. Years later, his work ethics and kind heart helped pave the way for him to earn a Council Member seat. He served in that capacity for years.

Uncle Simplicio did have a business mind and made money from rice paddies, fish and shrimp farms, abaca, fish traps, and of course coconuts. A cockfight arena in our property was open only during Sundays after church. A Filipino pastime, it was a hobby for him, for he had a collection of roosters of different breeds. I watched him from my bedroom window, training them to fight against each other, a game that I never cared to watch or be a part of.

I watched people gather around the arena, mostly men getting their rooster roused. The owner spit on the wings and gave the rooster a rub. Once it was ready to fight, they attached a two-inch kind of knife on one of the rooster's legs, and the two will face and charge each other. I can only imagine the rest because I never watched the actual event which I found disturbing. The roosters were colorful. I pet them once in awhile with sadness, knowing that on any upcoming Sunday the colorful and beautiful rooster will die or be a champion.

I really enjoyed the time we spent together hunting with Uncle Simplicio. We would go on a canoe trip, a riverboat ride along the Sibahay River hunting for ducks on our way to visit Pangingibiran, a forestland he owned where he lumbered beautiful teak and mahogany. I enjoyed it the most when the flock of ducks will soar in the air as we shot them with the shotgun in hopes of missing a shot until I learned the dozen or so little marble-like bullets would sprout all over for just one shot. I was so sorry for the now dead wild ducks floating on the river as we retrieved them looking at me, lame in their clear, watery eyes as if to say, "why did you do this to me?" I put my shotgun to rest in my safe bedroom.

In Hinangutdan, coconuts are the moneymaking food crop, but you can only harvest the coconuts every six months. Typhoons can damage or destroy the coconut trees and there may not be a harvest for a year or more. The coconut production is very labor intensive and tedious work. Workers will use a machete to put notches in the tree, which are used as finger and foot holds. Luckily, they can use the same notches at the next harvest. They need to climb to the top of these forty-foot trees to reach the coconuts. Once they reach the top, they take the machete from their teeth and chop the branch holding the bunch of coconuts and let them fall to the ground.

Once all the coconuts have arrived on the ground below, the picker will scoot down the tree to where the hard work begins. They will carry the coconuts in the protective husks back to the village. The mighty machete is the tool the worker used to remove the two-inch husk encasing the coconut. With the husk now gone, the worker raises his machete and lands it on the coconut, breaking it into two symmetrical halves. Now the halved coconuts are placed in a shack on bamboo slats with the pure white coconut meat facing down.

Since Filipinos are not wasteful people, they use some the coconut husks to fuel the fire required to cook and smoke the coconuts overnight. The next step in the process begins the next morning. The copra or white meat of the coconut is removed from the hard, brown coconut shell and placed on the street for drying, where it will take a day or two in the hot sun for it to dry completely. Kids used wooden rakes to move the pieces around and speed up the drying process. Once the copra has dried in the scorching sun, it is scooped into burlap sacks and ready to sell.

While the Island of Samar is beautiful, Samar is considered the poorest province in the Philippines, where I grew up with no electricity or running water in my uncle's home. We used the flickering light from kerosene lamps and lanterns to light the home and our drinking water came from an artesian well behind the church inside our property that my Uncle provided for the community. We also have a well just for us to use. My family home was full of fun and memories, but sixty years later, the home is gone, and the village is not the same.

To accommodate the increased population, homes now occupy the land where the fruit trees once circled our house. The wafting aroma of Ylang Ylang is now coming from people raising chickens and pigs where I once played with the other children. Even the birds chirping in sweet melodies are gone. The beautiful, bright, yellow and black orioles are gone. The path between houses that I used as a shortcut to Uncle Tito's home is now a fence made of bamboo and tree branches, probably to have privacy since they're so close together just like sardines. Only the fence separates the homes.

Tacloban was the closest place with businesses and going there was the high-light of my younger years. We loaded the sacks of copra or dried coconuts into a motorboat and made the two-and-a-half hour boat ride to Tacloban in a pier designated for small passenger motorboats. The pier was muddy and smelly. It was the central port full of hard-earning people wearing slippers or flip flops and carrying fish or sacks on their shoulders and other things. Vendors of some sort lined up along the edge of the water and across the dirty alley. This place had the most people who died during Haiyan where shanty homes lined the seawall.

Once we arrived in Tacloban, the sacks of copra were delivered to a regular dealer and good friend of the family, Mary and Pecio, Filipino and Chinese merchants. The warehouse was just thirty feet away from the pier, going through a narrow dirty alley just wide enough for two people to squeeze through.

Tacloban was the largest city nearby and the largest I had ever seen as a child until I was in high school and able to travel alone. I spent my holidays and some weekends in Hinangutdan. During summer break I visited Uncle Edelberto. I would take a flight from Tacloban a cigar shaped plane with a propeller engine under each wing. And the last year in high school, I went to a summer camp before leaving for college.

Uncle Simplicio and Aunt Cresencia would take me along to sell the copra, and we would stay for a day in Tacloban City. During our visit, we would visit family and friends and do some shopping. It was always a wonderful treat for me to visit Tacloban. Aunt Cresencia, with her Spanish features, was very beautiful and elegant. I never saw her hair down; it was always in a French twist. She liked to sew, and she made me beautiful dresses made from pineapple hemp and linen.

She was a tailor by trade, but it was a hobby to her. She would buy sewing materials by bulk during our copra trips to Tacloban. In addition, she'd stock up on things we did not have on the island.

As I got older, I always looked forward to going to Tacloban with some friends. We would go to movies, shopping centers, and Felisas Café where they served the best Halo-Halo ever. Halo-Halo is a cool dessert consisting of shaved ice, milk sugar, mongo beans, binagol or taro roots, coconut, caramel, and eggs. I never fail to visit Felisas Café when I am home for a visit. For over sixty years Felisas Café had withstood each typhoon that came and went. It did not survive Typhoon Yolanda.

I attended a private high school at Leyte Colleges in Tacloban. Close by were the boarding house, theaters, and shopping centers I frequented as a student. The entire area was devastated by Typhoon Haiyan or Typhoon Yolanda in the Philippines. Four decades after I left the Philippines, many smaller towns finally have a high school and Hinangutdan is no exception. This gives hope to the poor families that cannot afford to send their children away.

After Typhoon Haiyan ravaged Tacloban, the very boat dock I used for years to catch my boat ride home was destroyed beyond repair. This seaport and the seawall are now remnants of the past. The waves, at least three stories high, washed several cargo ships ashore as if they were rubber ducks in a bathtub. Buildings, businesses, homes, and everything else disappeared from the land when Yolanda was unleashed, but I pray Tacloban will recover in time.

It is now springtime 2014 as I write this, and debris still clutters the landscape in parts of Leyte and Samar. Sadly, dead and decomposed bodies are still being recovered from the rubble of Haiyan. My cousin Betty and her husband returned to their home in Tacloban in January 2014 from Quezon City, the big island of Luzon. They have started repairs to their home there. But electricity is scarce, so Betty returned to Manila until things are better. Some think it will take years for Tacloban to be functional again.

Countries and people from around the world pledged hundreds of millions of dollars and perhaps billions by now in aid. News reports seem to indicate the aid is not getting to the people that need it most. In addition, when the poor and devastated people finally get some needed relief, it is clear that the packages of food and supplies have been picked over. The government bureaucrats, rampant with graft and corruption are slowing down the reconstruction efforts and food distribution process.

An online article from the Filipino news agency ABS/CBN said the relief goods were sorted and placed in bags as part of a relay game during a track meet in Manila. They thought this exhibition was educational for the children, but it was full of hypocrisy and so disgusting to me when I saw the needs of the people after the typhoon. Lately I watched the ABS/CAN news TV Patrol Tacloban that found some of the relief goods in a Tacloban dumpsite, and more victims of the typhoon in the duress area are getting rotten supplies of relief, and extra worms added to the people's dismay, according to Ranulfo Docdocan's reporting.

Over the past forty years I have been visiting my hometown. When my three sons were ready to understand my culture, we all went with my husband to visit Tacloban, Leyte and Hinangutdan, Santa Rita, Samar. My husband and sons saw first hand the poverty I grew up with, how people lived off the land, and the poorest of people being happy. They experienced the boat ride I took many times between Tacloban and Hinangutdan.

They performed some charity work, gave food to the poor, and played with the children. Ian climbed a coconut tree and harvested a couple coconuts just like a seasoned coconut picker. The gents learned how to remove the coconut husk and notch it just enough so we could drink coconut water.

We were fortunate enough to have a vehicle and driver at our disposal. The gents were confused at why Islaw, the driver, honked his horn so often and kissed the cross of the rosary that dangled from the rearview mirror. The honk was a warning as he dodged cars, Jeepney, tricycles, and children playing in the streets. The roads were filled with potholes just like a slice of Swiss cheese, and he swerved left and right all the time.

We stayed at my cousin Betty's beautiful home. Servants met us at the vehicle and ushered us inside to the formal dining room, where they served the food the cook prepared earlier for our arrival. I observed the gents as we arrived at Betty's for the first time.

The gents (my sons) could not believe how big and beautiful this house was. Betty's hospitality was first class, and she had roast pig and seafood available each day. After a week of this fine food, the gents asked for a steak. Later that evening after dinner, I overheard Vilma asking Islaw, the family driver to take her to the market. I quietly asked Vilma if Tim and I could go along to see the market.

Around three in the morning, still dark, we hopped in the Ranchero as Islaw drove in the darkness. We approached the dimly lit market. The lighting in this place is very dim, which I assumed was because it is early in the morning and most of the lights were off. I was familiar to this and feeling relaxed, although, I feared for my foreign husband. It would take a week or more for me to get comfortable with my American family around Tacloban and Samar.

My awareness for my family had to vanish completely; we were only going to stay two weeks. Right now, being in this dimly lit market, I am still self-conscious. After all, this is a culture where the whole is greater than the individual, and I have just brought out a culture where the individual more important than anything else.

My family's first visit was with no understanding or speaking any Tagalog, our national language, or Waray, a dialect in Samar and Leyte. This is my home country, and I am responsible for them as my guest. Nevertheless, this is my homeland that I miss and love; I should be happy to share my culture with dignity.

A little way down in a dim corner, past the hanging undressed chicken and fresh fish line a man had set up a long wooden table slicing meat. Vilma approached the man and asked him to slice some for us to buy as he measured them on a scale. Almost everything there is measure with a scale.

At dinner, the gents were happy for the new menu on the table: steaks galore, meat with vegetable, meat stew, pepper steak, steamed rice, and fried rice. Our dining room was the place where all ten of us gathered, Boy seated at the head of the table opposite Tim, facing the double pillars hugging the smoke see through glass, as Tim sat with his back to the pillars at the other end facing Boy. I sat next to Tim in awe. What a big, happy family.

I remember our first dinner at Betty's in Tacloban. After Tim finished his plate, he picked it up to put the dirty plate in the kitchen sink, an American way of graciousness. The first day in Tacloban, Tim had his first treatment of royalty. Servants stopped him and asked for the dirty plate. I watched Tim with amusement, and he was bewildered. He politely handed them the plate without a word. Later he asks me what he did wrong. I explain. The following day and weeks we were in Tacloban, he learned quickly the life of the privileged in my country, where people are mostly poor.

Although for myself, I ache, crave, and dream for social change. For some odd, unknown reason, I keep on dreaming to solve, to find, the equation of humanity for perfection. It may not happen, but at least, my dream is to keep on trying.

We spent two glorious days venturing the private, small island of Dabong which is nestled between Hinangutdan, Samar and Babatngon, Leyte. We caravanned in two SUVs to Santa Rita on nice, sunny morning. We stopped at Betty's and Boy's home in Santa Rita, and the new group of servants welcomed us, waiting for our arrival. We approached the concrete, two-story Bungalow as the drivers parked the SUV along the side of the road next to the house.

As we walked in, AJ was behind me. He asked quietly, "They know we are coming?" as he smelled the food spread at the table ready for us to sit at. While the motor boatman is getting the motorboats ready, the servants gathered the food and other things we needed for an overnight stay at Dabong Island. We hung out at the municipal guesthouse and more food was served.

Soon after, we caught the motorboat ride from the Santa Rita pier. The water was perfect, not too choppy; it was a nice, short boat ride to Dabong Island. The motorboat is about twenty feet long and slender and bamboo poles extend outward on each side like wings. Dabong Island was visible from Santa Rita; it looked like a small island dot dividing Leyte to the left and Samar to the right.

I can see Hinangutdan on the horizon, tiny shanty homes along the seashore and a few two-story homes towering over them, patches of smoke billowing in the air probably from toasting coconuts, that gave the haunting aura of hardships inside the homes. The mountain slopes were covered with coconut trees. They towered toward the blue skies, the mangroves, and the whole community.

We slid the boat over Dabong beach. It is white sands from a distance, but walking on the beach, it was rough a mix of sand and seashells. Dabong was pretty and very private. The only unfamiliar faces were the caretaker and his at least dozen children. I asked. His oldest child was in high school in Santa Rita. The island had four mushroom shaped cottages made of concrete and the fifth made with nipa roofing and concrete bathrooms, a hundred winding steps lead to a grotto of Virgin Mary on top of the hill where I can see the panoramic view of the Canjabas Bay.

The other side of the island had mangroves full of wild orchids and a long, rocky point that looked like an airplane landing pad. The other side was the beach where we unloaded the supplies to a small, rounded shelter made of bamboo and nipa that was surrounded by a circular bench, at the center of which was the serving area. We cleaned the beach of debris and gathered fallen coconut tree branches so we could have a campfire after the sun went down.

We hiked around the coastline of the island in less than two hours, and our sons met the children of the caretaker on the island. These young kids, ages ranging from four to eight, showed the gents how to catch sand crabs with their bare hands. My gents were enjoying the nature, and it was wonderful to watch. During my last visit without my family in 2013, my visit to Dabong Island was not the same as when my family was here with me.

The waters around most of the island were shallow for at least thirty feet from shore, and you could almost walk around the island while in the water. AJ, walking along the shallow water, saw a tiger fish and yelled for his brothers to come. The yell startled the tiger fish, which charged AJ's foot, releasing a poison. I think his foot was a little numb, but okay in the scheme of things.

A couple people were roasting a whole pig over an open pit of coals. A bamboo shaft was inserted through the length of the pig and they sat for hours, rotating the pig over the hot coals until the pig was ready to eat. Roast pig is a welcome food for all occasions in the Philippines and even more so during the Christmas holiday season.

As the sun set to the west and the moon started to rise, our Filipino friends lit some lanterns for a little night fishing. This is very exciting to watch as these long, narrow, silver fish will fly over the water towards the lantern light. The idea is to smack the fish with a machete as they jump of the water. In the shallower waters you can see crabs walking around, easy prey for the little spring-loaded spear. None of this nice, sweet-tasting seafood went to waste because we ate them the next day.

I no longer have any immediate family in the Philippines, but my cousin Betty always welcomes me with open arms and a room, servant, car and chauffeur for my family. After that first family visit, they learned to appreciate my heritage. Brian, Ian, and AJ are very proud of being a part of Filipino culture. On the same island the morning after Haiyan, a body drifted to Dabong's shore, all the way from Tacloban.

August 19, 2013: I turned sixty-two. My husband, Tim, felt uncertainty for me to be away for a long period, though with reverence and support for my longtime dream. It was not a surprise for Tim that at this time in my life, I would consider putting a final addition to this dream. Tim, six years younger than me has to stay behind this time, but I hope when he retires we will work together on this most awaited dream for a cause, which he also supports and enjoys.

It was hard for both of us to think of my being away for a long period. After a rocky marriage with so much pain and suffering, we decided to divorce in 2005. I believe coming from two different worlds there was a lot to learn, so much misunderstanding, but God has always been on our side. Six months after our divorce, I was on my way to work, driving Sheridan Lake Road in Rapid City, South Dakota, the main road from our supposed-to-be happy home, where the children used to snowboard, drive the lawn mower in our backyard.

As I reached the top of the hill, I saw a woman driving a utility truck had lost control, and the truck was rolling to her right. I slowed down to wait for her to gain control as the truck started going uphill. The truck quickly changed direction and rolled onto my lane, hit my black 325i BMW soft-top convertible and dragged my car, with me in it, under the utility truck to an embankment. The Beamer was totaled and I was lucky for my roll bar, air bag, and seat belt. I was unscratched, just a sore ankle.

The first person I saw as I woke up at the Rapid City Regional Hospital emergency room was my ever-loving Tim by my side. He took me home and took care of me until I was well. The accident must have been a blessing from God—a renewed life for me, for both of us. We then lived together for two years, seeking counseling to resolve our cultural mix and complex previous marriage and to have a better understanding of both cultures for our happiness and the gents'.

I also asked him to come along, together with the gents (I call my already-grown boys gents), from Carlsbad to the Philippines and see my hometown of Hinangutdan in Samar, the first time for Tim, Ian, and AJ. Brian had been with me on one of my visits at eight years old and met my Uncle Simplicio. The reason was that I wanted Tim to know more about my culture and most importantly, my life growing up as a child and an adult that he never understood.

Our two weeks vacation mostly revolved around Tacloban, Hinangutdan, Santa Rita, the Tiopes privately owned island of Dabong, and a two-day visit to Calicoan Surf, a resort in Guiaun, Samar. The richness of nature and dire poverty was an eye opener for them.

After three years of being together, we remarried on March 23, the same anniversary date as the first time. Moreover, we have been supremely content, and the gents blissful. Furthermore, we have been in each other's company for church, outings, and even grocery shopping, a chore that is not on top of my list.

We sold the countryside home and bought a two-bedroom townhome in a nice, quite neighborhood with two full baths, a living room, and an adjoining dining room and kitchen. Our townhouse is just enough for the two of us, since the gents never come home to visit.

Tim helped me pack my bags and loaded them in the trunk of my champagne-colored Lincoln town car. The drive from our home in Auburn Hills, to the Rapid City Regional Airport would take about 20 minutes. Tim was poignant; after he unloaded my bags we hugged for the longest time as he emptied the I had mixed sensations at our parting. I had entered retirement and was excited to be with my gents in California for two weeks.

Carlsbad, California: before leaving for the Philippines, I spent two weeks visiting my three handsome gents. Brian Whiteaker, five-feet-eleven, thirty-seven, my son from my first marriage, has a fair complexion and a golden tan and is muscular—a black belt expert—and finishing his mathematics major at UCSD, California. He is a Nogi, Brazilian, and Wrestling instructor; he does the business part of Backline Training Center, a huge warehouse in the middle of the business center of Carlsbad.

The front desk as you come in has two offices to the right. A big door separates the gym. Inside the gym is a shower and bathroom and an arena with thick pads to train wrestling, grappling, and jujitsu. Next to the arena is a spacious, padded floor for kickboxing, kettle bell, and private training.

In Brian's free time, he will be out surfing at Carlsbad beach. He travels frequently to Rio de Janeiro and Costa Rica for the love of surfing. Brian's gym classes are more physical, with direct contact, so I pass. I did some strengthening at the gym with their retail products and staffed the front desk when everyone was doing their own thing.

Ian Matthews, five-feet-eleven, twenty-eight, is a talent coordinator for the Bellator MMA organization and a kettle bell instructor. He travels around the U.S., Canada, and once in Europe for Bellator, but he makes time to have a kettle class with me.

AJ, six feet, twenty-six, is a communications graduate at CSULA, a professional fighter for Bellator, kick-boxing instructor, and a personal trainer. He always wants me around, especially for his kick-boxing class. We would drive around Carlsbad, LA, to U.S. Route 101 and Laguna Beach in his somewhat put together red BMW. The reason I say that is, when I got to Carlsbad, it was partly painted, the door molding was missing, and some odd pieces still need to be put together, and the paint job was of rainbow colors. It was a work of art, but then it was his joy. In the two weeks I was in Carlsbad, it was like a metamorphosis. The day I left the BMW, it was like a brand new car—a sparkling, hot red—but not quite, the passenger side molding has a tendency to hang out from the door. His real name is Andrew James Matthews, and his screen name is Mercenary. You might see him on Spike TV, Bellator.com, and YouTube.

Beyond, the nice, sunny, sixty-degree year-round weather of Carlsbad, CA, that I like, I enjoy hanging out with them at their gym, Blackline Training Center, with their MMA friends and respectable clientele. I also have the pleasure of bonding with their women, Jess, Roy, and Steph. The gents, as I address them, would get pedicures with me, visit La Costa Resort and Spa, and request my home-cooked meals, to which I attach importance to preparing with love, for they hardly eat at home.

For Brian, sinigang na baboy—a sour pork stew with green vegetables. Ian loves adobo—a pork or chicken sauté in soy sauce, vinegar, water, bay leaf, and pepper. For AJ, lumpia—a mix of ground pork, chopped up carrots and celery, and a secret sauce, wrapped in a pilo. We call it lumpia wrapper. Some of their friends will come to the cluttered house, where a huge TV hangs on a wall and a comfortable L-shaped, tan sofa and round lounging chair frame a coffee table, the center of gathering.

The house is just a stone's throw to Carlsbad beach, so I would jog to the beach with my backpack for carrying the groceries on my way back home. Sometimes I would meet Brian at Starbucks for a cup of coffee at the grocery plaza. Brian loves Starbucks. It's his dream home, cool, he can read his math books, and there's coffee. The gents have lived under one roof for years, ever since AJ, the youngest, moved out from Rapid City to Carlsbad to join his brothers, when he was just in eleventh grade in Carlsbad High and preparing a California residency for college.

It is blessing that they all get along, and I thank God for that love, care, and support for each other. The gents were also excellent in sports, mostly soccer, that gave AJ the opportunity to get a full-ride scholarship at CSULA. Brian was their mentor, a noble son, instrumental in what they are now. He would take his brothers to a friend's garage, where for a ten-dollar fee there'd be mix martial arts training. On weekends, while AJ attended the University in LA, he would come home to Carlsbad with his brothers to train. Soon they became proprietors to a successful Backline Training Center.

Living in Rapid City, South Dakota, was hard for me, being away from my gents, but I try to save for my plane ticket two or three times a year for my priceless visits with my gents. It was as hard to say goodbye to the gents as it was to my husband, Tim, but I must move on to pursue my passion.

September 10, 2013: At six in the morning, Brian packed my suitcases in the trunk of his blue Acura and drove onto Melaleuca Avenue, left on Paseo del Norte, right turn Poinsettia Avenue past the I-5. A quick stop for gas and coffee at Starbucks, the only place Brian would get his coffee. In and out of the shopping center on to the long stretch of I-5.

The early fog from the Pacific Ocean was just rolling into the beautiful city of Carlsbad. I-5 is the busiest freeway, five to six lanes in each way that starts at the border of Mexico humming with cars to Washington State. The traffic was picking up as we approached the polluted smog of LA. Brian and I drove to LA, a two-and-a-half hour drive from Carlsbad. Brian dropped me off at the curbside of Delta Air and headed back to Carlsbad to teach a noon class at the gym.

Here I am ready to cross the continental divide, I approach Delta's curbside check in and show them my e-ticket; they took my luggage and went through the long line of gate security. I waited at the lounge for a connecting flight and prepared myself for the sixteen-hour flight to Manila, Philippines, before boarding the Delta Airlines international flight. I bought a fifty-dollar pass to use the Delta lounge for privileges, a cozy place, Internet, food, shower, and a quite room to catch some snooze for a stopover at Narita Airport. From my previous experience, Japan is the most expensive country to purchase anything. A fifty-dollar lounge pass is worth the money for freshening up for a long layover, especially at Narita Japan International Airport.

The loaded plane finally takes off and it slowly rises from the tarmac of the Los Angeles airport. Clear skies and into the thin air, clear as fine crystal over the clouds. This is a long time to spend cramped in an airplane seat, but I have done it several times over the years.

September 10, 2013: I arrived in Manila at 10:00 P.M., which I dread, to arrive this late. It was raining, sultry, hot, and humid. The smell of the tropics was welcoming, although in the city of Manila, I am always apprehensive in the airport, but even more so than ever late at night. People are asking for money as I try to make my way through customs. In an act of kindness, I put a couple dollars in my passport for the customs agent. She smiled, stamped my passport, and let me in to the country.

While I wait for what seems like an eternity for my bags to arrive, I went to the restroom. As I entered the restroom, I gave a tip to the attendant, and I was able to bypass the long line and entered the reserved stall. Amazing what a good tip will get you. I grabbed my carry-on luggage and ventured outside to find my cousin Betty.

It was raining hard and blurry as I crossed the dimly lit street, through the narrow, cement alley that unfolds down to the parking lot. The area designated for passenger pickup outside was dim, a hazy steam of people smoking combined with pollution. In addition, hundreds of travelers were looking for family members to take them home. I was a little apprehensive to venture out there, but I had to do it. At the edge of the parking are numbers of affluent people's cars, all with their drivers waiting outside smoking and leaning against them.

I nosed around with a bit of apprehension until I saw a woman rolling her suitcases and followed her down the dark cement alley. After an hour or so, I was very relieved when I saw Betty. I am embarrassed that she had been waiting and looking for me for quite some time. I did not have a notion that people waiting for arrival had to be outside the fence across the dark street. I waved at her as I ran back inside the airport to grab my suitcases and hand them to Lando.

We climb into Betty's SUV Ranchero while Lando, Betty's driver, shuffled my suitcases into the back of the SUV. We made our way out of the dark parking lot into the relentless, rainy night of the busy traffic jam of Rojas Boulevard in Manila. I was happy to see Lando again after five years, the last time I was home. He is an excellent driver. He has an average and no-nonsense look about him, quiet and had been Betty's driver for a decade, skillful on his way around Manila. I complimented him five years ago about his driving aptitude. The timing as he maneuvers the car amazes me, especially in Manila.

Lando dropped us off at the luxurious Dusit Thani hotel as the bellman rushed out to gather our belongings, and Lando drove back home to Quezon City.

My lovely confidante, Betty Tiopes, a remarkable woman with good taste, matching jewelry to every wardrobe, expensive shoes, and a large diamond almost as big as my pinky nail. She bounce as she walks but gracefully. Everything about her was of value. My cousin, a former mayor of Santa Rita, Samar, Philippines has a family home in nearby Quezon City, which is about two hours or more depending on traffic from the airport, but we had already decided to spend a few days for us to bond in Manila before going home to her home in Tacloban City. She conceded from the mayoral election that was held May 2013 for the time being, to be home with her ailing husband, Boy.

We arrived at the towering, beautiful Dusit Thani hotel in the middle of Makati City, the business center of the Philippines. We checked in at the counter, in line with beautiful people, looking like cats that just swallowed a canary and mostly young, women employees wearing long, body-hugging golden dresses, and the men wearing a Barong, traditional Filipino long-sleeve shirts made of fine fiber. The concierge assisted us to our hotel room, where the room's amenities were five star, spacious, clean, and accommodating, overlooking the pool, the poolside and the surrounding beautiful landscape full of lush greenery.

The hotel was an easy walking distance to all actions, businesses, hotels, restaurants, theaters are intertwining together, over the busy intersection below to next Mall above. Makati is the center of big business and towering skyscrapers like many large U.S. cities. Once we checked into our room and refreshed ourselves, we rode the elevator to an elaborate lobby with ornately carved moldings.

We take a table facing the garden near the poolside; the walls are a gold that matches the color of the employees' uniforms in the hotel dining room. Over a late dinner and drink, we talked and planned out our time in the hotel facility and the surrounding area for the next day's escapade. Jet lag set in at that moment, and I needed forty winks. On our way back to our room, I saw a spa sign and a Thai restaurant and a huge buffet flowing through about half of the lobby. I put it in my memory for a later visit. We rode the elevator and back to our hotel room.

We awoke the next morning and I was feeling rested and ready for coffee and breakfast. We checked out the fitness center for a little workout and the outdoor swimming pool. Afterwards, we changed our dresses and ventured outside, our promenade's destination being to the nearby mall. Across the beautiful Dusit Thani, I saw an unfinished high-rise, concrete blocks, an enormous pit, and stacked girders. We pressed on and finally came to an elaborate set of entwined pathways reachable by ramps, elevators, and escalators that connected the whole city of Makati.

We climbed up to find to a nearby café where we enjoyed a nice, relaxing breakfast of fresh fruits and bread. They have a collection of traditional breakfast items including dried fish dangit, ham, bacon, eggs, oatmeal, rice porridge, and pastries. I devoured the dangit as I dipped it in vinegar with crushed, fresh, tiny, red peppers with garlic-fried rice. After a long trek past fancy store after store with everything you could want in name brands from U.S. to European, it was lunch time. I saw the deserted stores early in the morning were now packed with people so that no one could move around. With the people sort of falling out of the doors it reminded me of New York. The site was incredible for a third world country.

The next morning we were back at the same place for more and they had changed the daily menu. I must have had a pitiful look as I glanced at the buffet table in awe. We were seated by the maître d' who walked away without a word. He must have remembered me because he ran back to the kitchen and came back with a tray full of dangit. It was funny though. Betty would desire foreign food and I have a predilection to eat the local dishes.

No matter how expensive looking Betty was, I always ended up with the bill, and I never understood why. Just a thought. I really do know what to call myself, but they call me American. I was in my own country, brown skin and all, but they are confused, as I am, about my nationality. It seems like I do not belong anywhere any more. We spent an enjoyable three days there, walking around and shopping and just relaxing. It was nice to enjoy good Filipino cuisine.

On September 14, another nice and sunny day, Betty and I visited the hotel gym for the last time and worked out for an hour. Back in our room, we got dressed and packed our belongings. Before we checked out we decided to check out the buffet brunch at the hotel. We took our time with the huge selection at the buffet, since we had a late afternoon flight and the airport was just minutes away from Dusit Thani. We did not need Lando, for we used the hotel transfer service to Manila Domestic Airport, a thirty-minute drive, and purchased tickets for the next Philippine Airline flight for Tacloban that was leaving in a couple hours.

I was so excited that I was on the last leg of this journey that would land us in Tacloban City where Betty's family would greet us. My home town of Hinangutdan was about within reach. I called the front desk to send the bellman to get our luggage for checkout. We were ushered out to a waiting airport transfer to Manila Domestic airport; it was a bit cloudy and the traffic was running smoothly.

As we ventured from the ticket counter to security I had to hurdle my fears of the poor people asking for money or food; I just wanted to get on the plane. The airport employees sensed something like dogs sniffing for drugs. Betty just had to ask, "Is it over the limit?" I knew for sure it was not. The counter person's eyes lit up and said, "Oh! Yes!" Now the drama started, and he asked for Betty and me to follow him to customs. Halfway to customs they had me wait by the fenced area. I was getting irritated with this treatment. It turned out to be fine, but it gave them a chance to steal few of my things.

This bothers me out each time I pass through. I removed my ID tags from my bags so they could not tell I was from the U.S. and ask for money. They think everyone in the U.S. has a lot of money and can give it away. I kept an eye on my bags as they traveled down the conveyor belt and through the wall. So far so good and my bags did arrive in Tacloban; however it never fails that some items were removed somewhere along the way. I am remorseful to mention this about my home country, but it seems to happen every time.

The domestic airport was being refurbished or worked on and it was crowded. Every hour there was an announcement: a group of fifty people or so would get up like a flock of geese to go to a waiting shuttle and leave. Then another group would arrive and the room would be crowded again. After an hour of waiting for our flight, it was announced for boarding. We caught a shuttle to take us to the Philippine airline tarmac. The hour and forty-five minute flight was nice and smooth; it was stunning peering out the Plexiglass window to see all the islands. I could see patches of inlets and sparkling blue waters around the islands.

After the plane ride, we were now in Tacloban City, Leyte, the historical monument where the bloodiest decisive naval battles of Leyte in the Philippines happened during World War II. This is where the amphibious invasion of the Gulf of Leyte by the Americans and Filipino guerrilla forces under the command of General Douglas MacArthur, who fought against the Imperial Japanese Army on the Island of Leyte, occurred.

Leyte has numerous deep waters and sandy beaches. The historical site was badly damaged by Super Typhoon Haiyan. The lowland extending inland along the coast of Tacloban to the north and the San Jaunico Strait between Leyte and Eastern Samar. The Leyte northern coast to the long eastern shores contains most of the towns.

Haiyan continued its wrath south to the port of Ormoc and then along the western shore, mostly along the path where Filipinos and Americans faced the harsh repression against the Japanese forces. In addition, the same path Yolanda/Haiyan took. San Pedro and San Pablo Bay provides a coastline to Western Samar and Eastern Samar.

Tacloban is nestled in the northern part of the bay and is somewhat protected from the Philippine Sea by Samar, but the elevation is just slightly greater than sea level and vulnerable to storm surges or tsunamis and is typically hot and wet throughout the year with frequent, heavy rainfall.

Tacloban, the capital of Leyte, had grown during the past decade into a tourism hub and the gateway to the Eastern Visayas. Economically, Tacloban was one of the fastest-growing cities in the Philippines. It has one of the lowest poverty incidence rates in the country at roughly nine percent (the national poverty incidence stands at thirty percent) and is the richest local government unit in the Visayas.

Tacloban Airport is the key transportation hub for the Leyte and Samar region. Located at the tip of Tacloban City's small peninsula, one side is San Pedro Bay and the Leyte Gulf toward the open water of the Pacific Ocean. Philippine Airlines descended to the airport tarmac on nice, clear, sunny, and humid day. The newly refurbished, rectangular airport structure was gravely damaged by the storm but the landing tarmac was usable and useful for the C-130 to land to deliver relief goods and for the transportation out for the Haiyan's refugees.

We landed safely and I was almost home again to a sunny Tacloban. Betty's son, Paul John Tiopes, has two distinguishable facial expressions, a sweet young lad or a grouch. There is a sinister look about him with his thick, bushy, black hair, brows thick like Boris Karloff's, pouty lips, and husky (on the chubby side) frame. He's tall for a Filipino and the youngest of five siblings, nicknamed "PJ." He still lives at home and is a fulltime college student. He was majoring in engineering like his dad, Boy. PJ and Boy met us at the airport.

Boy's real name is Menandro Tiopes. In his sixties, he's a very smart man, quiet, reserved, and attentive. Most juniors (named after their father) in the Philippines is called Boy, a pet name. Betty handed our baggage claim to a porter so he could get our luggage. I was nervous to leave my personal belongings with someone I did not know. We waited at the black SUV Fortuner. The airport porter got our suitcases and loaded the luggage into the trunk of black SUV Fortuner as we climb in; PJ drove us to the Tiopes residence, which is about fifteen minutes from the airport. We made our way out of the congested, airport gravel parking lot and on to the full of activity of Tacloban City.

One of the first things I saw was a row of colorfully painted Jeepneys parked along the side of a wire fence, the drivers talking, laughing, and smoking while waiting for passengers, hustling and bustling. Jeepneys are the most popular means of public transportation in the Philippines. Their known for their crowded seating and cheap and flashy décor, which have become a ubiquitous symbol of Philippine culture and art. Each owner will paint and embellish his Jeepney, as he wants meaning and for no two to look alike.

The passenger section of these jeepneys consists of two bench seats running the length of the Jeepney with an aisle, enough for a thin, Filipino body to hunch down as you look for an empty seat between them. The driver will pack in as many as he can like sardines for the reason that means more money. I have seen them so full that people and goods actually pack the roof, too. Tacloban, though a snappy city that' supposed to be a fast-growing city in the region of Visayas, the city has a desolate, cold, famished feeling to it.

There is the odor of salt in the warm sea breeze as the sun beats down upon us. We drove along the shoreline of San Jose where most of the poorest reside in shanty homes. After the Haiyan, thousands of dead bodies beached ashore like driftwood and some lay under the debris. The vast stretch of vendors under a shade made of bamboo and nipa palm were selling young coconut juice and some Filipino pastries wrapped in banana leaf and fruit stands in every corner of the smelly, muddy, rough sidewalks.

The coconut leaves are swaying in the breeze, mixed with polluted air and dust that seemed to clog the air from the skirting Jeepneys which do not come to a stop. Rumbling alongside a few cars are trikes that are like mopeds with a sidecar and canvas roof. They are dodging the potholes and people walking in the street. There are not many rules about driving there, so PJ took his time and honked a form of warning whenever he'd make a move to not hit a pedestrian or something. Some of the streets branch like spokes of an oval wheel.

After about ten minutes we turned off the Main Avenue and head up along the Maharlika Highway to the eastern coastline of Tacloban. Before we reached MacArthur Monument we saw a new hotel called Oriental. It is painted white and very pristine looking and has an Olympic-sized swimming pool. It used to be a government owned hotel, General MacArthur's namesake, and past Macarthur Park where years after the war ended, this beach area was turned into a national park. General MacArthur waded ashore to liberate the Philippines and offered his famous promise, "I shall return."

Houses line both sides of Maharlika Highway. Some are dilapidated and rundown and they are gray from dust and pollution. We pass an amazing-looking new home, which I dub a "giant rooster" the front is painted in all bright colors; it was so amusing to see. The existence of poverty is obvious, the city still the same even though there are new buildings standing next to a rugged home with telephone and electrical wires dangling. The sewer and canals are open and always clogged with garbage and smell badly.

After a few more turns we enter the V&G Subdivision. Giant mango trees are everywhere and Betty lives on Mango Street. Land is scarce, so houses are built next to each other with very little breathing space between them. The streets were filled with potholes that made PJ swerve left and right and to avoid mud puddles from the recent rains and scraggly stray dogs that whip away as fast as possible. The condition of the animals is standard; there is no place yet for an animal rights person. It would just drive them mad.

He came to a stop in front of the soaring double gate of wrought iron above broad, stone steps that provided an entrance to Betty's home and four two-story high pillars. He honked the horn twice and a family servant swung the heavy gate open and we drove in.

We drove up to the two marble pillars that held up the veranda above, a monumental shelter that would soon save our lives. He came to a halt on the pebble stone garage floor that provided shelter for cars and we got out of the black SUV. Before us was a wide garage that was also used for parties and entertainment with television. An iron grill separated the outside kitchen from the main house.

As I emerged from the SUV, I noticed Vilma Lacambra majordoma (the head of the family servants and cook), bounding out from her kitchen domain. She has been with the family for years. Vilma has curly black hair with brown highlights. She limps when she walks, for she has scoliosis, and I saw her coming toward us. Ever since I first met Vilma I admired her kindness. Her kind face, so evocative of wisdom, sensitivity, and suffering, perches on her thin and imbalanced posture. Her clothes were mostly rugged, similar to someone losing interest in herself. Maybe she was tired. She was a good person and a friend and had never been married, and least I think she's in her mid-forties. It had been a long five years since I saw her last. She was happy to see me. We hugged each other then went to the side door to the left leading inside the luxurious rambling two-story home.

The construction business has prospered for Boy. It was the time for the old V & G single-style homes to be pulled down and to make room for the sprawling two-story house of Boy's own design combined with Betty's taste of class. It had a peaked roof and was set on a piece of large property for an area where building space was limited.

A tile-roofed house with wide verandas and spacious rooms paneled in undressed mahogany wood and the finest marble floors and glass windows surrounding it from floor to ceiling, the house defied all architectural rules, not blending into the neighborhood but showing Boy's engineering endowment and proficiency in his construction business.

A ten-foot tall cement wall circled the property for personal safety and I honestly believe this wall provided some fortification from the tremendous 235-mile per hour winds of Haiyan. Between the wall and the home was a lush green manicured yard with an assortment of colored flower gardens and a multiplicity of trees and orchids of special breed. A path made of red tile brick lead to the rear, ending at the swimming pool to the back of the house.

At the corner of the yard was a secret covered patio with overhanging trees, making the patio cool and refreshing. The birdsong is almost as deep and soothing, a theme of shipwrecked pirates' collections adorned the patio. Ten steps away from the grotto of Virgin Mary was a wall of seven sculpted dwarves that screened a shed for garden tools. In front of the grotto was a miniature dewpond with Kio fish swimming around and a collection of water lilies and a dancing water fountain in the middle.

The white pillars outside that support the veranda above the recessed, red tile floor entryway which leads to a heavy ten-foot tall double doors made from mahogany wood. The house sat like a huge rectangular pediments atop a gatepost. I walked through the front doors. The entry floor had an inlaid circle design of colored marbles and another two marble pillars welcoming us to the beautiful sitting room, where the ceiling was two stories high.

The whole house was all a light pink that infused a sunglow from within, the gleaming pink marble floors and flushing capability. It was quite pristine and displayed substances that Betty had collected over the years: furniture made of beautifully carved teak wood, a mini bar below the winding staircase, a study and music room leading to master bedroom, and Steinbeck piano in one corner.

I walked up the spiral staircase that circled around the hanging, taupe colored, glass chandelier to the second floor. At the top right corner of the staircase was a beautiful six-foot-tall porcelain vase. At the top of the winding staircase to the right was a sliding glass door which I opened and walked through to stand on a veranda that veiled secrecy around the backside of the house. The view was breathtaking: mountains, lush in greenery, trees and towering coconuts in the distance.

However, as I look down adjacent to it, rows of small houses had either just been completed or were under construction with rusty galvanized rooftops and unfinished, dilapidated, old homes. As I looked around over them, a total disparity of the standard of living shot my heart to my throat, making it hard to swallow.

This veranda also served as a partial awning for the swimming pool below, wherein at high noon, sunlight has room to shine. There was a lighted waterfall, a mermaid sculpture on the middle of the wall decorated with hanging vines and orchids, and two sets of steel furniture painted in white for outdoor sitting in each end of the egg-shaped swimming pool. A sliding glass door opened from the entry room to the pool.

Glass from the floor to the ceiling filled the wall, covered with window trimmings made of expensive draperies lined with white organza all over the home. The other side of the house faces Mango Street. Two giant mango trees were on each end of the street. There were two more verandas and one had a pool table.

The second floor of Betty's home had three separate sitting areas with three different colored pallets and unique theme. Each one displayed a collection of colored glass vases, stone figurines, and porcelain dishes. As I entered the first sitting area there was a six-foot-tall ballet dancing girl in porcelain and blue-colored collectibles. The second was a pink color collection with a five-foot-tall glass tree, and the third collection was green.

All have matching colored chairs and sofas made of carved teak wood. Facing the huge bay window, the two double bedrooms both had two full-sized beds and a separate large family room where the children would play or watch a limited number of TV channels. In addition, there were two more bedrooms and a utility room on the second floor.

The spacious attics had two additional bedrooms for the staff, a wall lined with wood closets, and a large storage area. A stairway leads to an always locked, low-ceilinged, private office room, encased by a glass wall and door were three office tables and a computer with Wi-Fi. The office in the attic, with the kitchen and servants' quarters below, had a glass window facing the monumental wrought iron gate.

Downstairs were a master bedroom, secluded music room, and a formal dining room for ten people, which had a view to the swimming pool with some lush greenery hanging the wall. During special occasions the pool and waterfall were lighted in blue, emitting an aura to the luxury of the home.

Two alluring marble pillars embraced smoked glass which was etched with fish shells and fruit and surrounded the formal dining room. A swinging door allowed easy access for servants. This room is painted in gold and was also full of fine China and the collectibles are gold in color. Phenomenally, the room was saved from the storm.

A door and a sitting room for privacy on the left of the formal dining room lead to the alcove nook that leads to a kitchen (that was hardly used) and the alcove nook where we mostly had our meals served. All the main rooms had mahogany-paneled walls and wood-carved doors. Brightly colored Oriental rugs were scattered on the polished marble floors. The hallways were wide, lined with tables covered with vases and some flowers from her garden.

The house is too large for Betty and Boy now that the children were gone, living on their own. This home was one of the few with running water, indoor plumbing, and electricity in the neighborhood. A pump on the ground pumped water to a plastic reservoir on the roof where the water was warmed by the sun and provided water for a shower, washing clothes, and watering the plants. I stayed up visiting with Betty for a while after we had dinner and got ready for bed in the guestroom she always gets ready for me. And I felt good and very much at home.

The Tiopes residence is like a mansion and the central point of the subdivision. At one time, I ask JR to drop me at the Robinson's mall about four blocks away from the house, and I told JR I would venture on my own and take a public transportation. I triked back to Betty's. The driver asked me where I was going, and I told him the address. He did not know. I panicked. Well, I told him the biggest house in V & G, and he immediately signaled me to get in.

I think I had a blind eye as I never noticed or paid attention to the level of poverty until I walked out on the second floor veranda facing the mountainside and the city of Tacloban, overlooking the Pacific Ocean for the first time. My cousin Betty offers her generosity when I visit a guest room a car with a waiting chauffer at my command whenever I'm in Tacloban and Hinangutdan. I am also thankful that Betty's luxurious house had provided a huge oasis of safety and comfort to withstand most of what typhoon Haiyan offered.

Sunny and calm today, after a day of rest in Tacloban, I packed a few things for my few days stay in Samar. This is the trip I have taken in hopes of overseeing the construction of my resource center to keep lasting memories of my departed family. JR was now my personal driver. His real name was Narceso Cajefe, short about five feet tall, well built, a crew-cut with spiky, thick, black hair, and a round face with a charming smile. He was married with four young children ranging from newborn to four; he cannot read nor write but can text.

JR and I stopped at a nearby shopping mall, Robinson, minutes away from Betty's home. A brand new mall and over crowded, it was still very nice and advanced, the first of its kind in Tacloban and air conditioned similar to our stores in the U.S. A two-story building, the grocery store was huge with a food court in both floors. The mall is well stocked on the first floor with cosmetics, a pharmacy, groceries, and restaurants. On the second floor are appliances, TV, computers, Internet cafes, more clothing departments, and cell phone stores, smart and global, same as Verizon.

Robinsons Mall was impressive. For the first time in Tacloban they had something of which to be proud. There were escalators and it was very noisy—in the middle of the store. They had some live show or presentation of some kind. JR got a cart as I walked in front of him to get a weeks supply of food before heading west to Hinangutdan. The grocery baggage boy gathered my groceries while JR went out to park the car at the grocery entrance.

JR put the groceries in the back of the Ranchero and drove out of the parking lot. A very short-lived convenience. Once you get out of this main road, you're back to the *Twilight Zone* with more potholes, traffic jams, and pedicabs, tricycles, jeepneys, pedestrians appeared in each direction. We made our drive to a public super market by the seawall past downtown Tacloban; it was a nightmare to find parking and we had to squeeze in a tiniest possible space you can.

This part of Tacloban was where you found more of the poorest people trying to make ends meet. You cannot help but notice some people and young children walking without shoes or slippers, working like a freelance porter, carrying crates of fish on their backs and sacks of copra. It saddened me. Nothing much has changed since I left forty years ago.

JR finally saw a pocket of space to park the Ranchero. I disembarked and went to a rice vendor. The rice was sold in kilos or sacks, but I had to select from an array on display and decide the price point from smelly rice to premium. I bought two sacks of the average price and JR carried them on his back, hunching as he held one end. The market was in full swing. You have to hold your nose (for it is also smelly) and watch your step.

For sale are roosters, raw meat, eggs, eels, vegetables, clothes, and house wares and packs of tissue, a necessity for a country in which toilet paper is scarce, all packed together in a narrow alley. I bought a cooler for my raw meat and some fish to bring to Hinangutdan. Bicycles and pedicabs are miraculously squeezing by us. To have your own transportation is a luxury to only a handful of them.

We drove out the main road to Maharlika highway crossing the San Jaunico Bridge. At the foot of the bridge on the Samar side was Santa Rita, seventy miles of unending coconuts and bananas with houses attached to the highway and vendors were common. The town proper was about an hour of smooth driving. A blacktop highway ended until we could turn left under a welcome archway to the central town of Santa Rita, where the never-ending potholes began.

From here on, the road is terribly bad. It is hard for me to convey. Imagine I could use all the nouns and pronouns, still you will not understand, trust my word.

Camayse is the first Barangay leading to Santa Rita, the center of the official business trade and government buildings for the township. The only consolation is a breath of fresh air and the aromatic scent of the vegetation from the farmland. It is rice paddy farmland, with an occasional water buffalo plowing or a farmer bending over picking or maybe weeding rice plants, endless coconuts, bananas, and few vendors along the road.

The setting was sylvan and beautiful. Occasionally you would meet an ancient water buffalo tugged by a rope in his nose with his master guiding him along. There were shanty homes at the edge of the narrow highway, barefoot young children, chickens, pigs and dogs walking about. The roads were super narrow, very skinny, and an odd combination of cement road with dirt in between and deep potholes.

JR was a clever driver, an expert on driving different terrains. He managed to dodge swamps and big boulders along the way. He ran over a dog crossing the road and never even stopped or blinked. I was sad for the poor dog. Locals that live along the road use the already narrow cement road for drying rice and copra, and he just drove over them.

We made it through the four-wheel-style driving and arrived in Santa Rita and continued on to Hinangutdan. The road was even worse with deep potholes and erosion. The cement road looked like sand pebbles, and more coconut branches blocked the all-terrain road, neglected and truly rough. I thought about visiting the local TV station to complain about some unfinished roads that were supposed to have been funded. The local reporter Ranulfo Docdocan and his signature jungle hat were out to see the road, and he was planning to visit the Santa Rita local government. I am so happy to know that a television station is now in Tacloban and that a reporter is very much concerned for the benefits of the people. I admire his spunk.

The Ranchero climbed a rocky hill past the public cemetery. Minutes later, we emerged at the Hinangutdan waterfront. Two more private cemeteries were to the right and left as you entered beneath the welcome archway for Hinangutdan by rich landowner property by the Canjabas Bay to Hinangutdan. I can hardly believe that they allow a private tomb in their property.

It was now noon and the sun with its powerful shining seemed to sting my skin. Hinangutdan looked the same. People dressed the same. There were a few additions of concrete home next to a shanty and an unfinished home towering behind the church. Yet it's still a typical reminder of poverty as I look around from the tinted car window. My heart ached and I broke down sobbing. I am always moved whenever I am home. My emotions poured out of me that had been aching for years. Respite from poverty, families, love, in many cases life itself.

The beauties of this land made me appreciate more in life and helped my heart long ago, the special luster of the seaboard and mountain peaks. I remember years and years of walking on the muddy rims between the rice paddies, the long, slow *moo* of my pet water buffalo, his huge nostrils flaring, the long black eyelashes that framed his giant face, the yoke eternally around his beautiful neck. I felt relief now because I was trying to do something during my six month stay. Sadly my stay would be shortened by Haiyan.

It was around two that day, hot and sunny, when we arrived. It was dead quiet and hot. The people must have been inside their homes napping or out farming. No children were running around in laughter. I arrived at my nephew's home (Jojo Cajipe), a good-looking man, about thirty years old, where I arranged to stay before my arrival. I had only seen him briefly during my short visits. There was no Jojo at the comfortable beach house, but the door toward the beach was wide open. I looked around, but I saw no one. I summoned my bravery and looked inside, walking in easily.

I finally heard footsteps from behind. As Jojo emerged from the loggia, he give me a big smile that showed his missing front teeth, wearing torn, baggy shorts and no shirt. He was very skinny and I could see his bones, like the ones you see in a picture hanging at the doctor's office. He had never married and seemed happy to have my company and I liked him a lot. Since childhood he had impaired hearing and wanted to buy a hearing aid. He had long shaggy hair and dark chocolate brown skin.

In addition, he looked sharp whenever he dressed up in a white Blackline T-shirt and new, white Nike shoes that I purchased for him as a welcome gift. I might say he was a good and efficient cook. The home belonged to his parents. His mother passed away, and his father lived in Santa Rita, where they also have a family homestead.

A pleasant concrete-built bungalow, the home was square, painted in green and white, and unpretentious, concealed by wooden fence and two guavano fruit trees from the street. I had a chance to try the fruit, nice and sweet, its milky, white fruit sap and leaves are known to cure cancer. In front of a wooden gate secured by a rope was a well where we fetch our water for washing clothes and bathing. We bought bottled water for cooking and drinking.

Single-petal gumamela swathed around the front to the entryway to patchy Bermuda grass. There was a shade tree on the beach side where I spent most of my time writing in my journal. Funny thing about this house, Jojo lost his key to the front door., He never replaced the lock and never found the key, so when we were not home, we asked the neighbor Henry and Marilyn to watch the front door, and the back door was locked.

Henry and Marilyn have a few children in the house, but I never had a chance to meet them. They were very quiet and private. They supplied me with vegetables from their garden and other root crops from the farm. Jojo's house has two bedrooms. My bedroom was toward the front with no key but could be locked and my bedroom door was screened by a curtain. The bed was made of bamboo and after a night of sleeping on the hard bamboo, it was time for me to invest a five-inch-thick cushion for my sore body.

I brought a mosquito net that we hung from the ceiling when I was ready to settle. Jojo's bedroom was next to mine and had a broken door that never moved facing the kitchen. Luckily, he was slender and able to slip in and out. His small living room was furnished with bamboo chairs, a TV, and a stereo set that was also nonfunctional adorned one side of the living room. On top of the stereo cabinet was an altar to Jesus Christ.

The dining room and the kitchen were in one room. All the windows were made of glass shutters. A loggia made of stone and corals wrapped around the kitchen and dining room, facing the Canjabas Bay. Around the corner by the kitchen sink was a very small bathroom with no shower but a tub full of water and a stall with a tank that Sonia kept full. I was happy for Sonia Cajipe and her son Tintin, a fifth grader. He too was staying with us.

Sonia is thirty-five years old and my cousin Dondon's wife. Dondon and Sonia were separated. Dondon lived in Florida, U.S.A. She was about my height but on the chunky side with round face with short hair. Her energy was big and positive; she had the straightest nose and almond eyes. I was very happy with her and never saw anyone like her. She talked loud to enable her to communicate with Jojo. Sonia was there as much as necessary for the times when it was hard for me to communicate with Jojo.

I got pleasure from Hinangutdan, for there was not a single mosquito, although the beach was polluted. During high tide the water would reach our doorstep. Jojo's home was only ten feet away from the water. Every morning we had to sweep out the beach driftwood, plastic bags, and some other stuff pushed by the waves to our yard.

On clear nights, in spite of the folklore of (aswang) witches and fairies around Hinangutdan, I would sit outside after dinner, when almost all the community was in bed, just to cool off and relax before going to sleep. I watched the stars and listened to the waves gently rolling in and about the beach as I sipped my wine and wished my husband were with me to enjoy the peace and quiet evening without television that I never missed for the two months I'd been here.

The effervescent moon would spread its blue rays to the bay and make the lapping waves look like diamonds glittering. The shadow of the mountainside was mysterious and intriguing. The quite evening lent clarity and a haunting, melancholy beauty. One night Sonia and I were sitting outside at the loggia and there was no breath of wind. This evening it was very still and balmy.

A bat, in noiseless flight, swooped and flittered across the shade tree to the loggia and was about to land on my head. The sudden swish sent my heart into a panic and purple willies in me. Sonia flicked the ugly bat across in front of me and he was gone. Sonia then warned me that I may be haunted and charmed the old Filipino folklore *aswang* that put a spell on people as they hunt for victims at night. That was the end of my dreamy night sitting at the loggia.

Electricity has finally made its way to Hinangutdan in a limited and undependable way, but it is better than no electricity. Running water in the houses is still a dream here, so people have to fetch water from a well close to the house. The (pogon) is a Filipino cooking stove made of cement blocks, and is fired by charcoal made from coconut shells.

Coconuts are considered "The Tree of Life." The trunk is used as lumber, the leaves are woven into roofs for shanty homes, the nuts are used as copra oil, the shell for charcoal, and the husks are used in various ways, woven into mats and even to start a fire for the pogon. I enjoy the pogon, but starting the fire will put you in tears from the smoke. Once it's started, say goodbye to your French manicure. Your hands and fingers will be all black from the charcoal as you fill the fire until you're done cooking.

Next time I will bring my own gloves for the sake of pogon. On the days we are providential enough to have electricity, people will use the electric rice cooker to make the rice and an electric water pitcher to boil our drinking water and make it harmless. Some are privileged enough to have some amenities of the West, like a refrigerator or electric fan.

A few days later, nice, sunny days, it seemed as if it is my luck was to have this nice weather, to visit the municipal engineer to survey my property before I start my construction. I was happy for Santa Rita, Samar. Now we had a beautiful gymnasium, a new and well-designed market by the bay, a guesthouse, and the Santa Rita Municipal Building had been renovated and had some wing added to it. I was honored to see all these improvements. The municipal hall was still in the same location as it was years ago when Uncle Simplicio and I used to visit.

The entrance to the government business in Santa Rita was a narrow, open space to a rugged parking lot with a flagpole at the center of the building. To the left was the guesthouse. The center of the police station and the jail were behind it. To the right was the main government business building. There used to be some towering trees by the entrance but now they were gone. I entered the narrow entrance lined with plastic chairs where people were sitting. I climbed dark, narrow steps to the second floor as I passed small offices to the small, congested, ten-by-ten offices of the municipal engineer. There were three small desks for the engineer and his assistant. I made an appointment for him to survey my property and paid my yearly tax.

I got it all planned out; I hired a contractor to put a fence around my property for my Resource Center/Library. I was back again to Tacloban to purchase the supplies along with the contractor and his list. We arrived at the hardware store before noon. The contractor turned in the list, and then we had to come back after lunch. The hardware store closed for an hour for lunch, and I was amazed.

So we were back. I sat at the utility truck while the laborers stacked the steel bars, cement, hollow blocks, barbed wire, chain link, and other supplies. The warehouse was dusty from cement and smoking. My heart ached over what I saw. The manager or owner was wearing a mask, and the laborers was left to die of lung disease, young men working without shoes and masks, no shirts, the working environment was appalling. I learned that laborers earned from 250 to 300 pesos a day, equal to $4.50 a day. There were more labor laws to be concerned about, a learning experience that was hard to accept.

October 14, 2013: A month later, mid October. Sonia and I went to Tacloban, shopping for food supplies in Hinangutdan and decided to stay overnight. We checked in at the hotel adjoining the Robinson Mall (the first of its kind in Tacloban City), since we would be shopping there the next day. It was nice one-stop seaside mall for shopping for groceries, clothing, and hardware, with a movie theater and a bank.

In addition to complimentary wireless Internet access and refrigerators, guestrooms feature air conditioning along with safes and coffee/tea makers. The room was small but comfortable with small shower with hot water. Therefore, I decided to treat Sonia, my helper, for her services, for dinner at Don Vicente, where we planned on what to prepare for the coming fiesta. She was appreciative, since by no means has she ever been in those places before with a chance to sleep in a soft, comfortable bed rather than the hard cement floor at Jojo's home.

I was woken up by a swaying movement. Then it stopped and it did it again. I did not wait for the third movement; I realized it was an earthquake. I hurriedly spun around, grabbed the duvet, wrapped it around me, and ran out. I left Sonia. Minutes later I saw her coming with my bag and my iPad. There was a group of people gathering at the hotel courtyard looking uneasy.

We waited for a while until the hotel management informed us that it was safe for us to go back to our room to collect our belongings. It was an earthquake indeed, 4.2 in Tacloban. In Bohol, the epicenter, the 7.2-magnitude earthquake devastated part of Bohol Island in the Visayas region in Philippines. Landslides and aftershocks pushed people out of their houses and tents, while flooding and heavy rains drove them back to unsafe homes, according to the news.

It was my first wild vacation experience. Little did I know there was more to come and I would be at the center of it. That was a daring occurrence that left me flinching. In the late 1960s, I was in high school in Tacloban when I first experienced an earthquake and an enduring, irrational fear had begun. I got so nervous, I could not be alone for months. The phobia that been healed soon to come back to haunt me. Every day after the earthquake I had that feeling of the earth moving under my feet, a fretfulness I could not shake. I had to be with some company always. That same day we finished our shopping and drove an hour to Hinangutdan, Santa Rita, Samar.

October 16, 2013: Another fiesta and Hinangutdan was perfect, just perfect for the occasion. The sun sat high in the powder blue sky. The daily temperatures had been hovering in the mid nineties, but it seemed cooler with the breeze coming off the mountains. I was getting deliriously hungry from the yummy aroma of roasting pigs as it entered my open bedroom window. The golden brown, crunchy pigskin is one of my favorite things to eat here. I took a small piece, dunked it in vinegar and hot pepper sauce, and put it in my mouth. I savored each taste as I began to chew. Delicious!

My relatives wanted that event to be special, so I let them plan a little party for us. We had two people as guests, Norma and her friend, during this time. You cannot plan on how much you would serve. Everyone will just show up for a visit, eat, drink, and be merry all day. Early morning before Mass, we already had company, my favorite aunt, Bigida Ariza, a retired school principal of Santa Rita, the last surviving matriarch that I could remember. She passed away after the Typhoon Haiyan, and I will miss her so.

She brought her two young grandchildren from her adopted daughter, Marissa Cajefe, who is JR's wife. In addition, there were two police officers and a co-worker of my relative Renato. Good thing we bought plenty of eggs, bread, and spread. It was fun. Everyone was preparing pancit, chicken adobo, for some reason they loved spaghetti, steamed rice, and roasting pig in the yard. It was automatic; everyone knew what needed to be done without talking. It reminded me of my childhood days growing up with Uncle Simplicio.

At nine in the morning the church bell was ringing. The Mass was about to start, so I left everyone cooking and went to church. The Mass lasted an hour, followed by a procession around Hinangutdan under the scorching sun. The procession was lead by the celebrant and followed by group of women wearing pink, holding streamers of Virgin Mary's portrait and followed by the icon of Virgin Mary, decorated with fresh flowers in a push wagon and the priest behind.

Following the Mass was a luncheon at Shirley Tarrant, the Patron Saint celebrant's home. Shirley, a widow Filipina that resided in England, was home for this occasion. She was slim with a mouthful of teeth and very long hair. The luncheon was huge, under a canopy with about fifty round tables covered in white tablecloths and a long presidential table where I was seated with the priest and other special guests.

Night came and it was time to change. We could hear live band music echoing from where we had lunch. I put on my purple, chiffon, below-the-knee dress with matching accessories that I brought just for the occasion; I put my hair up in a French twist. The live band music started playing oldies rock and roll and some Spanish tunes of rumba. It was as if memories were back, and it was time for us to go the charity ball. I was seated again at the presidential table with no other special guest seating with me. I must have drunk a bottle wine myself, and Shirley stocked wine on my table that no one attempted to join me.

Everywhere in Hinangutdan was walking distance and this one was just forty feet away from Jojo's house. All the women, Sonia, Vilma, Norma, and I attended the festivities, which were the highlight of the fiesta. Norma, a friend I met through Betty, had been inviting me to her family's farm. We had some special Filipino delicacy: a fresh harvest of young rice toasted on a wok under a fire. Once they pop like popcorn, put it in a wooden mortar and pound with a long and heavy wooden stick until the rice is flat and separated from the shell. Put it in a large bamboo pan and shake it to separate the shell and the already flattened rice. After that process, put it back into the wooden mortar and mix with young coconut and sugar until they are fine enough to melt in your mouth.

The charity ball was to raise funds for the celebrant's expenses. The leftovers go to the church. During the charity ball, they would spread a huge handkerchief (that look like a sarong for me) in the middle of the dance floor where everybody threw money, the minimum limit of P20. In addition, anyone who wanted to dance with their choice would also pay. The fiesta lasted for three days; I got to see some relatives attending the fiesta. It was great to see them again.

While in Hinangutdan, besides overseeing the fence project for my resource center, I also had adopted four school-age kids, Angelica (14), Wilbert (13), and identical twins Joan and Jerralyn (10). They stayed with me, and I helped them with their daily school routine. Their parents lived nearby and they just come and go. I enjoy being around children. They are innocent and eager to learn. Adults friends are more pretentious and want more from you. I wanted to learn from these children, going back to my childhood. I went to a sporting goods store in Tacloban to see what they have.

I bought playthings for them: a basketball, badminton sets, a volleyball and net. It should keep them busy when out of school, and most importantly, I wanted to buy a hula hoop for me. I felt like I was gaining weight from eating everything I saw. I bought a half dozen so I could have fun with the children. It was so nice to see these children happy, learning English as I read books to them and learn from them. I had some children's programs in my iPad, games and reading. The iPad served well as visual entertainment, for we did not have TV or radio.

On a nice evening, we would roast marshmallows with their other siblings on our sandy beach and tell stories. After school, the kids in the neighborhood would come and play with my adopted children. We had plenty of room in our beach set up for a net for volleyball. Others would do the hula hoop and badminton.

In the mornings, before the sun started shining its orange glow on the horizon, I jogged around the two main streets in Hinangutdan. On one early morning jog, I saw a line of jugs and people waiting for their turn to pump the water from an artesian well. I noticed that the pump was loose, since a part was broken. It was tied by a rope to secure the pump. I asked if there is anything I could help with, maybe replace it with a new one?

I asked if I could have the missing part to bring with me to Tacloban for replacement. The hardware store in Tacloban recommended that I should buy the set, about 8000 pesos (equal to $200). The following day, I brought the new pump. To my surprise, it was already replaced by a running Kagawad candidate. So we replaced another artesian well that had been idle for quite some time.

One circumstance, I invited my childhood friend Nonita Canete to give me an idea about on how to cook some sweets, just about everything I could think of that I missed during the years I was away, a total reminiscence of the past. I kept myself busy working, clearing the uprooted jackfruit tree that had been on my property for over sixty years. That poor old tree was still producing fruit, but I had to make way for putting a fence around my Resource Center, I saved some cocoa and coffee trees.

I attended Sunday Mass to discuss what they might want done to the old church that needed maintenance. It was hard for the five groups of organizations to come to an agreement on what needed to be done. I merely listened and waited.

My once a week visits to Betty in Tacloban were to talk to my husband, Tim, in South Dakota for updates on our weekly activities and to catch up on our children in California and my Facebook friends. I went to visit Tacloban on Wednesday where Betty, Boy, and I would go to a Redemptorist church for worship of our Mother of Perpetual Help. I loved the church, which was where I used to go while in high school. I'm not sure how old it was, but it was one of the oldest churches in Tacloban. The monumental church with colorful stained glass windows overlooking the Pacific ocean was used as an evacuation center for Tacloban residents during the fury of Haiyan The church structure remained standing. The rest are beyond repair.

A week before Haiyan (international name for Yolanda), it was nice and sunny. I decided to go to Tacloban for my church business in Hinangutdan was not coming into place. I thought I'd stay there until Betty and I would go to Manila for rest and relaxation. I bought a ticket for us for November 8. While in Tacloban, I decided I would take the Tiopes family, along with JR and Vilma for a brunch after church at Raphael Farms a mile or two from Tacloban, a place for family outings with separate buildings for different venues designed for the occasion. The architecture is all made of traditional Filipino materials: capiz, nipa, bamboo, and wood located in a valley full of beautiful greenery and horses, a walking path, a paddleboat lake, and a huge tree house. That beautiful place was ravaged by Haiyan.

Prior to All Souls Day, I packed a few clothes and toiletries for the days I would be in the town of Santa Rita. I stayed at Betty's concrete single-story house with a one-car, pebble stone garage with a sitting area of wood furnishing—a nice, cool place to sit on a hot day with a nice breeze coming from the Santa Rita Bay. Inside the outdoor kitchen was a dark, taupe, marble floor, a recessed chandelier, glass windows protected with wrought iron grills, a nice-sized living room, a small bar, and a small hallway that leads to the dining room.

Six steps lead to the master bedroom on the left and a guestroom to the right. The bedrooms each had a bathroom and one downstairs and a basement below the bedrooms. A thatch-roofed house with a veranda above the garage overlooking the San Juanico Strait, the caretaker a single mother of five, Belen.

Belen was a stout woman who never smiled. Her below-the-shoulder-length hair, full and curly seemed to fit her being. She had been with the Tiopes family for years, and I am like family to Betty so they serve me with outmost respect. The home barely moved from the strong winds of Haiyan. It was also circled by a six-foot wall with greenery hanging between the house and the wall and at the corner a grotto of Virgin Mary.

The house was a short walk to the cemetery located at the northern end of the town; the streets were rugged, open canals with weeds. The scary, bony, stray dogs looking for food and sniffing the smelly garbage concerned me the most. Betty's home in Santa Rita was convenient during the days that were spent preparing my family's gravesite for All Souls Day.

Sonia and I cleared the spider web of vegetation that had over grown the area. The gravesites consisted of concrete tombs that are above ground and rest in a small shelter. The vines and weeds cleared, the tombs and shelter were painted a brilliant white.

November 2 2013: Finally, All Souls Day arrived. It was nice and sunny, and the celebration started with a mass at the cemetery chapel. When the mass had concluded, people made the trek to the family tombstone to honor their departed family members. My first time ever attending was a pleasurable moment for the deceased, a time spent with family and friends while people called upon others and had a good time.

By noon, the crowd was thick. Vendors built a makeshift store along the side of the narrow and rocky dirt street to the site. They were selling anything they could from food and drinks in a plastic bag with a straw already in it to handmade brooms. The Santa Rita Public Cemetery is very near the rock-strewn summit by the Bay and off the main road is a passageway to the chapel in the middle of the cemetery.

To get to my family's gravesite was like a jigsaw puzzle on this day. The tombs were placed in an unorganized manner. It's easier said than done for people to make their way to their resting family members. Because of the way the tombs were developed and the thick vegetation in some areas, people would climb on top of the tombs and jump to the next one so they could carry on their way.

People brought food for their family, friends, and of course, the departed. The day transitioned to night and candles were lit at the cemetery to provide just enough light to see the people. This had been a very interesting time for me, since it was my first time to witness this festival. I learned you were supposed to go to other gravesites and visit, but I chose not to partake. Later that afternoon it started to rain. We walked to a nearby Bakhow beach for another traditional party for All Souls Day.

November 3, 2013: It was sunny and breezy in Santa Rita. JR and I drove to Hinangutdan to pick up a student, the first-class graduating valedictorian from the National High School for a tour of the University in Catbalogan. It was a two-hour drive over the zigzag mountainside from Santa Rita.

At the mountain peak, we could see the Catbalogan shoreline overlooking Makeda Bay. Our day's drive was overcast and gloomy, we checked in to a nice, cozy hotel, Casa Cristina, in busy, downtown Catbalogan. My first time in Catbalogan, Samar brought happiness and sadness to me. The province itself is so beautiful, but once you look at the people, their existence is raw. How could the local government be so blinded? Rule if you must, but do not let your people down. I only hope that after the wrath of Haiyan, everyone will someday wakeup and realize that material things are not priority. We should be glad we been given a chance to live to better ourselves for a better future.

Samar Island is where Ferdinand Magellan laid a sovereign hand on the archipelago for Spain and introduced Catholicism to the natives long ago. Samar province is the third largest island and has mountain ranges and some of the greatest annual rainfall in the Philippines. Catbalogan, the capital of Samar, faces the beautiful Makeda bay. It has breathtaking waterfalls flowing down the mountain; hidden lakes and exotic wild life are just some of the natural beauty of Samar Island. Moreover, Biri Island has rock formations and coral reefs in the area.

Downtown Catbalogan has narrow streets congested with trikes. It was like a swarm of bees all over in every direction, unlike Tacloban where there was a variety of public transportation. There, I had my first meeting with Oscar, my Facebook friend, who, along with his family, tirelessly donated his time, choosing to help me distribute my SMC Educational Fund good tidings.

Oscar Maribojoc, a polite and nice looking young man about my son Brian's age, was a government radio station employee; he had his own program for lonely and heartbroken young adults, providing answers and playing requested love songs. His wife, Jessebel, was also about that age, a charming, shy, young woman with a beautiful smile, long black hair, and who was been assisting Oscar and me with my programs for gift giving, feeding street children, school supplies, materials and scholarship awards. They had two boys, Taba (10) and Payat (8).

JR was somewhat confused about the directions to their place the "Carinderia," a small eating stand with two entrances inside the bus depot compound. We drove around a few times on a stormy, rainy day, till Oscar came waving out in the middle of the bus depot and the downpour stopped.

To the left of the 20 foot square Carinderia as you entered was a display of cooked food consisting of pancit, adobo, fish, and a display of knickknacks hanging on the side and a pot of rice. There were four small, square tables and white plastic chairs, a fan, a small TV, and a narrow stairway on the corner that lead upstairs above the Carinderia, where they lived along with their two young lads. We had refreshments, they served a Pepsi and bibingka, a rice pastry on a banana leaf, and after a short visit, wrapped some dried squid for me for take home. I asked Oscar and Jessebel to join me for dinner.

It was almost 6:00 P.M. and cloudy. Oscar and Jessebel recommended the Balay-Balay Restaurant by the bay for dinner. We all got in the Red Ranchero, and JR started his skillful maneuvering away from the trikes. Pedal driven, they were fun to watch. They pedaled in unison like a flock of birds, so no one could take over and shielded each other from their competition, the colorful jeepneys.

Just as soon as we embarked, the thick clouds hovering over Catbalogan started to pour hard along with strong winds. Balay-Balay was an extraordinary place. There were single huts and apartment-like buildings divided into rooms with karaoke machines. We had to pick the apartment-like room for dinner, for the wind was blowing hard, and the rain was mightily pouring. I think we ordered almost everything on the menu and some to go. The room, food, and Karaoke were paid in a certain amount and time.

November 4, 2013: The following morning it was not raining but the thick clouds were still looming. We checked out of the hotel, we met Oscar Maribojoc and his wife, Jessebel, and I, along with my future scholars met with the University President and registrar to get some information for the school programs and facility. After a few hours touring the university, we stopped for lunch at JC Food Stop, a Filipino McDonald's. We had a selection from rice to hot dogs.

Afterward, we dropped off Oscar and Jessebel at their Carinderia, drove around Catbalogan, which remained crowded with markets, shops, and more pedicabs humming around us. Stumbling over rubble and uprooted street cement,we found our way out to the Maharlika highway, then headed out back to Hinangutdan.

November 5, 2013: Inadvertently the storm was looming over the Pacific Ocean, although I never noticed anything of concern from the locals. In contemplation, I seized the benefit of visiting Guiaun, near the southernmost point, after reaching the mountainside of Basey from Santa Rita. The underground river lead to Sohotan Cave in Basey, Samar and to Borongan on the Eastern coast of Samar, where the notorious Typhoon Haiyan, whose wind peaked at around 315 kilometers per hour, first made landfall and would relentlessly swipe the Visayan region completely and touch off in Vietnam.

The Samar and Northern Samar provinces were spared by the typhoon. Our drive to Guiaun was nice and sunny with clear, blue skies. This beguiling part of Eastern Samar promised a tropical scene. There was always a new beach where the warm ocean breaks and slides over the sand; it was so beautiful with blue skies and tranquil, blue ocean waters. That day I did not see a sign of ghastly, ominous weather.

I visited my only brother, Boy, from my mother, the raison d'être. I never have acknowledged that she ran off with his father. I met Boy briefly for the first time thirteen years ago during a short visit to the Philippines. He was anxious to spend time with me to learn more about the mother that both of us did not know. For at a young age (at four years old), he and his older sister were also left to their father's care.

Boy met us at downtown Guiaun where the streets were even worse than in Catbalogan. It was crowded with pedicabs. He arranged a hotel room at the Guiaun oceanfront Marcelo Hotel with a floating restaurant where the waves touched the floor. Looking in between the wood floor gaps, it was like a reflecting pool. It was so clear that you could actually see the corals and fish swimming. We enjoyed dinner as the gentle, blue ocean water of the Philippine Sea rubbed the restaurant floor as the waves bounced back from the seawall like a shower.

My entourage JR and Joevir (five-foot-five and overweight for his height), a schoolteacher from Hinangutdan, stayed overnight since it was a four-hour drive back to Tacloban. We toured around the beautiful Guiaun. The shoreline along the blue Pacific Ocean was breathtaking. My family did not get to see the beautiful shoreline in 2006, since we would have had to drive a ten-hour detour though the mountains.

The regular road was damaged from the previous typhoon and landslide. My second visit was unforgettable; the famous Sulangan Church was now newly refurbished from a small to an immense cathedral. It even had its own miracles that it was famous for; Haiyan did not trouble it.

We drove to the tip of the peninsula, the Calicoan Surf Camp, the place we visited in 2006 with my husband and sons and the Tiopes siblings: Garrett, Sheryl, Sandra, Christina, and PJ. That beautiful resort was not an exception to Typhoon Haiyan's raging ocean waters. The siblings were able to communicate with my distraught husband and children during and after the days that we were helpless in the devastated Tacloban.

November 6, 2013: Early the next morning, my brother Boy arranged a breakfast for us at his home a few minutes drive away from the ocean. A lone, beautiful, gated house nestled in a meadow. The home was large, an above average for the neighborhood. It was an open space and comfortable home. As you come in, to the right was the sitting area and to the left, the dining table and a doorway leading to the kitchen.

The housekeeper, a woman in her late fifties, lived in and served us breakfast that consisted of fried rice, fried fish, eggs, sausage, fresh fruit, and young coconut. After breakfast, Boy, JR, and Joevir went to the market to purchase some fresh fish, for Guiaun was known for its ocean fishing grounds, while I stayed and visited with Joan Carey and her newborn baby, a Filipina with an Australian father and Boy's housemate. They brought back a cooler full of giant squid and large, ugly fish with thick skin that I had never seen before. After having some of the fresh coconut water that we brought with us, we collected our things to head home to Hinangutdan to drop off Joevir.

It was before noon when we left Guiaun and still nice and sunny when we started our journey back. We stopped for a late lunch at Caluwayan Resort in Marabut, Samar, facing Leyte Gulp, another tourist attraction. There were few tourists but it was not as busy, since it was the middle of the week. This resort was overlooking some rocky inlets that looked more like where the James Bond movie *Golden Eye* was filmed.

It had single cottages and a hotel under a beautifully landscaped coconut grove, a swimming pool shaped like a figure 8, and a small walking bridge. While waiting for our lunch, Joevir and I rented a canoe. It was very hot, but there was a good breeze on the water and we were alone. The bright sunlight glinted off the sea, making it look as though it was covered with diamonds. To go around those inlets looked dreamy. The water was calm, a nice time for short canoeing around the rocky inlets.

I love staying fit and maneuvering the kayak around was a superior exercise. It was hard to imagine a storm was already gathering up its strength over the Pacific Ocean. This beautiful resort was a promising asset to Samar economy, the poorest province in the country and was in dismal situation during the Typhoon Haiyan. After paddling around, I was now panting when we glided into port.

It was time for our lunch and there were only two huts occupied in this paradise. Joevir and I pulled the canoe onto the beach. Joevir was at the front and as soon as we reached the beach he got up and jumped out with full force, not knowing I had my left foot out in the water. The canoe was made of fiberglass and swerved to the right so quick that I was not able to control my body with my left foot out. I lost control and fell into the water.

Oh God, I prayed as I sank into the ocean floor in agony, do not let my knee be broken. I cringed in the water; I could barely talk; it was an excruciating moment that I was not able to get up. I sat there, my body half immersed in the water for about twenty minutes. I glanced at my knee, and it looked bruised. I sat longer in the seawater above my waist until I felt relieved from pain. I limped to our lunch table, angry with myself that my left knee had just recovered from a Sumba twist and now this.

The sun beats hard and afterward, thick, gray clouds slowly covered the scorching sun. Subsequently the breeze followed with a downpour. I changed my drenched clothes at the resort restroom and ordered our lunch. As soon as we finished and paid the lunch bill, we left, as it was windy and about to rain, and drove back to Hinangutdan.

November 7, 2013: Alarming Call. Tacloban in the early hours of the muggy morning. My knee hurt a lot and was a little bit swollen, but did not feel like it was broken. I was planning to make an appointment with the doctor, but I was worried it might just get worse. Before breakfast, I Skyped my husband, Tim, and told him about my canoe accident. Moreover, the forthcoming super storm that nobody cared about. Every place I went, everyone was nonchalant. This typhoon, super storm Haiyan aka Yolanda, sounded really bad as it approached the Philippine waters the last time I watched ABS/CBN TV Patrol Tacloban.

The TV weatherman looked so serious and very concerned, reporting the 315-km typhoon. Meanwhile, Vilma was switching the channel to a game show of some sort so I asked Tim if he had heard anything about the approaching typhoon. He had not heard anything about it, but said he would check.

Tim

November 6, 2013: After I completed my Skype call with Emy, I then notified our sons Brian, Ian, and AJ, that a storm was to hit the Philippines with winds of 250 mph. Brian thought it was probably 250 kilometer per hour (155 mph). I messaged Emy to verify the speed, and she agreed with the 250 kilometer per hour, and she did not seem too worried about the coming storm.

Jokingly I told her to head for Japan. After we said our goodbyes for the night, I went to the computer to see about the storm headed for the Philippines.

8:09 P.M.	Messenger: Tim and Emy after our Skype call
	Tim: Is the typhoon 250 mph or kilometer per hour
	Emy: It is 250 per hour.
	Tim: That is too much. Brian thought kilometer per hour
	Emy: He is right. Sorry.
	Tim: Be safe! Night
8:50 P.M.	The last Facebook (FB) post by Emy as Yolanda approached
	Here are the stats, Brian Whiteaker Ian Matthews AJ Matthews Tim Matthews
	Signal #1: Camarines Norte, Camarines Sur, Catanduanes, Albay and Mindoro provinces. Burias Island, Romblon, Marinduque. Calamian Group of Islands and Southern Quezon. Aklan, Capiz, Iloilo, Antique, Guimaras, Negros Occidental, Negros Oriental, rest of Cebu, Siquijor, Misamis Oriental, Augusan del Sur.
	Signal #2: Sorsogon, Masbate, Ticao Island, Northern Samar, Biliran, Bantayan & Camotes Islands. Northern Cebu including Cebu City, Bohol, Surigao del Norte, Camiguin, Surigao del Sur, and Agusan del Norte.
	Signal #3: Eastern Samar, Samar, Leyte, Southern Leyte, Siargao Island and Dinagat.
	#YolandaPH

After a few minutes on the Internet, I learned this was going to be a huge storm and that much destruction and devastation would follow. I was now scared for the people in Tacloban, especially Emy and her family, and I tried to contact Emy again, but could not. This was the start of several sleepless nights and long days. I felt stupid for not hearing about Haiyan sooner. Perhaps I could have warned them ahead of time.

Emy

Tacloban: I shrugged off the disturbing news, went to the secret patio and read a book from my iPad. I thought Tim would be able to tell me. Later, he talked to our son in Carlsbad California, Brian, then immediately called his dad saying that maybe it was kilometers and that would be strong. Tim, after he confirmed the weather channel and saw in the news himself, immediately called me back and warned me to get out of town. Now there was a storm signal #4 and the direct hit would be Tacloban. Jokingly I told him, oh sure, I am on my way to Japan.

Actually, I had a flight reserved for the following day, November 8, for Manila. I did not see any urgency from Betty and Boy, and I shrugged my husband's word of warning. Aside from the looming weather, that Thursday November 7 before the storm seemed like any other day. I could hardly get up; I was not feeling well early in the dark morning. I woke up with a nagging headache and a sore throat.

My knee was swollen from the boating accident and ached whenever I moved in a certain way; it was throbbing with shooting pain and I cringed as I made a step. I got a call from Michelle, a distant relative. She wanted me to go on an outing with her, Felix, her live-in lover, and their young child. They lived a few blocks from my cousin. If I had gone with them, I could have missed the dreadful days or been caught in the middle of nowhere to hide for the storm that was about to land.

I slowly got dressed and gathered the things I needed to save time from climbing the stairs every few minutes. I limped downstairs to join breakfast with my family. We always had fried or steamed rice in the morning with dried fish, corned beef sautéed in garlic and onion, sweet potatoes and bananas, fresh fruit and bread. And at breakfast, I was now eating light. I must have gained ten pounds ever since I arrived, so I had coffee and bananas.

Eerie Cries of Dogs: after breakfast, I helped Vilma clear the table and trod slowly to the secret patio to wait for a call from Sonia as to where to meet her and the children from Hinangutdan to have lunch and shop. As I sat there reading a book and drinking my morning coffee, I listened for the birds that usually began chattering at four-thirty; there was none. Then I heard an eerie cry of dogs across the street that gave me goose bumps. I walked lamely across the street, looked over the gateway to the neighbor's house to see what dogs were howling and would not stop. Not a soul was around. That was enough for me to get spooked and I think it took me half of the time to walk back, and I forgot my pain.

There is stillness, as I sat unaccompanied at the patio only the pitter-patter of rain hitting the roof, but yet it is hot and humid, and I felt lifeless, like sitting inside the sauna. I had been here for weeks now. I never paid much attention to the time, one day folded into the next. I was losing track of time. I received a call from Sonia. I went to the house and asked Betty for Vilma to come along for a day out.

We got into the red SUV, a six seater with more room in the back for the children to cram into. JR drove us to meet Sonia and the children at McDonald's at downtown Tacloban about fifteen minutes away. As I looked around, nothing was really out of the ordinary in the busy downtown Tacloban. Everyone, shoppers, store owners, were just doing their own thing. At the McDonald's located at the pier that used to be the jeepney parking, were the drivers who used to be waiting for passengers, chatting, smoking and laughing.

Across a crowded shopping plaza was the busy the downtown Tacloban, where you saw endless little shops under canopies. Inside was dark and musty where everyone chattered like birds and loud music competed for each stores sale announcement. Sidewalk vendors stands clogged the sidewalk; people were elbow-to-elbow with no worries. It was windy and cloudy, but the dark, orange sun would peer in and out from the thick, gray clouds. For some peculiar reason I sensed a doomsday was about to come.

There was not any panic at all or announcement for everyone to leave and take shelter for the storm that was about to arrive. The city was business as customary. It was just like an ordinary happening, but at the same time, there were warnings on the TV and radio. Local officials had downplayed the massive typhoon as a storm surge. Still no alarm from the local government, but if it were on TV, the weathermen's reports could have saved lives had they translated the real meaning of storm surge as tsunami.

Although they did advise to evacuate to a seaside Astrodome, which later I found out that when the first wave rolled in, people panicked and wanted to run out. Once the door opened, some were washed out. As the second wave followed, it carried more out. It must have been like a washing machine cycle; I can just imagine how it was after the third wave roll in. The local government set up rubber boats and advised anglers not to go out to sea. I saw shanty homes tied to a coconut tree or a big rock. There was not any urgency at all. The children, Sonia, Vilma, and I finished lunch, and we headed to our shopping. JR was called back home and was not able to join us for lunch and forgot to fill the SUV with gas.

We walked into a wonderfully festive, two-story, unorganized store. The clothing department alone was an explosion of rainbow colors, including sundresses with little sun hats to match, all tacked up on a wall. The styles were simple, very childish, and reminded me of my pretty dresses made by my aunt. The dresses had long sashes made into a bow at the back of the waist. At one corner were stacks of shoes and some on the wall. I let the children choose, with the help of a sales clerk. The sales clerks were wearing blue uniforms and heavy makeup. They looked like china dolls.

Later that day it was gloomy and the wind was blowing, but it did not stop everyone from going out and about. After a long day of window-shopping, we stopped at Shakey's for lunch at the pizza place, the restaurant was packed and normal. The children ordered chicken, rice, and spaghetti. Vilma, Sonia, and I ordered a large pizza and we all had soda for drinks. We packed the leftovers and sent them with the children to take home. Who would have thought a catastrophe was just around the corner?

Betty and Menandro, "Boy," and the rest of the household I was staying with was not even worried. I was merely riding along with their own discretion, for they would know better. However, they have been through a lot of typhoons, an average of twenty a year, and were immune to the upcoming situation. On the other hand, I warned them to board the glass windows, and JR pulled some of the breakables and rolled up the Persian carpets in the entry room. There were so many things to put away.

The storm surge Haiyan was gaining its momentum as time went by. Betty, my cousin, and her family were confident that nothing bad would possibly happen; the house was almost a mansion with manicured, land-scaped gardens inside the monumental Iron Gate. There were high walls bordering from the neighbor's smaller houses.

At both ends of the block were two huge mango trees. Later, the mango branches reached out across the street, electric posts and wires hung loosely. Some old, some new from different companies that none of the companies would claim, because the bumpy road was narrow for a two way street. The house withstood with minor problems. Some tiled roof collapsed and glass windows and doors shattered.

Meanwhile, the tropical depression that became super-storm Haiyan was gaining strength over the Pacific and being monitored around the globe. Except the impoverished part of the Philippines, all were in full force; it was considered one of the worst typhoons on record that formed over the Pacific Ocean. On November 5, 2013, metrologies were soon able to announce to people that a storm was on its way. On November 7, evacuations were underway along the shoreline in the region.

Some were mislead, a tsunami was about to reach Tacloban on the eve of November 7. My niece, Edith Aguilar, who lived at PHHC, told me afterwards that they evacuated to the mountains nearby PHHC, a housing project along Maharlika highway. That same evening, they received a flashing signal that it was okay for them to come home. All along the shoreline, Guiaun, Samar, Tacloban, Leyte, Ormoc, and Cebu were at particular risk. However, Guiaun and Tacloban City were surrounded by water, which was so vulnerable for storm surge.

Congested shanty neighborhoods built along the seawall, many of which housed the city's poorest and most susceptible people, were at risk. The day before Haiyan hit Tacloban, Mayor Alfred Romualdez issued an evacuation order. He also declared that the Astrodome, a stadium located relatively close to the water in Palo would serve as a shelter. By nightfall, the elderly, mothers with young children, and some 10,000 had sought shelter in the Astrodome.

Thousands of others chose to wait out the storm at home. Given the warnings, Sonia, my helper from Samar, and I packed the children into a car for the hour drive back to Santa Rita and returned home and then went back to the store with Vilma, the family servant, to get five days of supplies to better weather the storm. The grocery store was busy and most had a cartful of food supplies; it was somewhat unusual for it never was that busy at previous days.

We stopped at the pharmacy to get some cold and pain relief for me and went home. If they had said Tsunami, we would have run for safety in the mountains. I lie awake in a rising fury, I do not exactly know what to do, but trust the hostility will blow over. Can this be happening? I hold out at home in Tacloban, believing that the storm will pass us by. I have to catch a flight for Manila the following morning. Little did I know I would be stuck in the darkness for five days with no sense of the outside world, where my family was distraught, not knowing of my whereabouts or the terror that followed.

U.S., meanwhile Tim is now very much concerned:

10:20 P.M.   Tim's Facebook post:
                Philippines are going to be hit by a super typhoon. Leave, Emy, leave. 160+ mph winds.

10:46 P.M.   Emy's Facebook comment to my post:
                I am heading for Japan.

That was Emy's last post for many days, and some people thought she left for Japan, but I knew she was joking. I knew she was in Tacloban the day before the storm but was not sure if they left prior to the storm to head somewhere else. I went to bed, said my prayers, and tried to sleep.

November 7, 2013, Thursday:

I awoke early, turned on the TV, and did not find any news about the typhoon, so I went to the computer to see what I might find on the Internet. The weather reports were describing an event so huge that this could very well be the largest typhoon in our history. It is Super Typhoon Haiyan. The storm had not yet hit land, but would later today. I left for work with a worried heart.

7:27 A.M.   Kristina's Facebook post

I miss you my ever so handsome and crazy little brother...!
Love you — with Pj Tiopes.

10:23 A.M.   Tim's message to Emy
Darlings get out of there. It is getting stronger. While at work, I searched the Internet for news whenever I had a chance. Yolanda hit Guiaun, Samar around 2 P.M. our time. I left work at 4 P.M. and headed home. As soon as I got home, I turned on the TV, and the Weather Channel had the best coverage at this time. The eye of the typhoon would engulf Tacloban very soon.

4:12 P.M.   Tim's message to Emy
Darling please call if u can

4:37 P.M.   Tim shared a Facebook post by Joyce Meyer Ministries
Our prayers go out to those in the Philippines as they endure Super Typhoon Haiyan, one of the most intense typhoons in history. Please pray with us!

I was glue to the Weather Channel and CNN all night as I waited for any coverage of Tacloban. Videos of the wind and rain were horrifying. I do not believe there was any coverage yet of Tacloban, so I went to bed, said my prayers, and hoped to sleep.

I think Brian called in the evening, wanting to know if I had heard anything. "Nothing yet," I said.

November 8, 2013 Friday

6:09 A.M.   Tim's message to Emy
Darling it is a day after the storm. I hope all of you are ok. Please contact us when u can. Praying for you.

My sister, Marcee, called me as I was eating breakfast and watching the news. She wanted to know if I had heard from Emy. I said no, and that I was not surprised that I had not heard from her yet. Marcee said there was only one death reported so far.

6:45 A.M.   Tim's Facebook post

No news out of Tacloban yet as all communications is down.

9:29 A.M.   Brian's Facebook post

I am waiting to hear from mom...That super Typhoon's eye went right over her.

3:50 P.M.   Sandy's Facebook post

Do not have any news back home. Last heard from my mom this 4:30 A.M. (11:30 P.M. here in Doha). I can even hear the strong gust of winds on the background when I called her. Even just a network signal make, it happens so I can reach them. Dear God, please keep everyone safe in Tacloban.

6:21 P.M.   Tim's Facebook post

Tacloban airport was destroy yesterday.

9:59 P.M.   Tim's message to Emy

Darling where are you? This sucks please come home.

I would keep sending Emy messages every day just in case she was able somehow to view them. She did not see them until she arrived in Manila a week or so later.

I think this is the evening Emy's sister, Erlinda, called me to see if Emy was still in the Philippines. I said yes, she was in Tacloban, and I have not heard from her yet. We would talk or text daily until I heard from Emy and knew she was okay.

Another night glued to CNN and the Weather Channel looking at the Filipinos in the videos to see if could spot Emy. No such luck. I went to bed, said my prayers, and tried to sleep.

Emy

November 8 2013: Typhoon Haiyan struck the coastline of Guiaun, Samar and Tacloban, Leyte, Philippines. When the storm made landfall, it had the Category 4 rating. It brought sustained winds of 200–315 kilometers per hour and stretched out some 1200 kilometers across. It would ultimately kill 5,290 in its wake, with more than 1,000 missing. The tempest itself did an enormous amount of damage, but its repercussion was cataclysmic.

Some people charged that the Unitary Government was too slow to meet the needs of the people affected by the storm. Some may have fled and some have drowned with their families. No news from the local government; the mayor was nowhere to be found. The following day, the mayor and his family were safe at their family beach resort Patio Victoria in San Jose.

Hundreds of thousands of people in Samar, Leyte, Cebu, mostly of the Visayan Region where displaced from their homes, and experts estimate that Haiyan caused more than $100 billion in damage. There was no way that Super Typhoon Yolanda (Haiyan), barreling at 315 kilometers per hour across the Visayas and affected provinces could be avoided.

The strong winds woke me up in the early hours of daylight. The tempest Haiyan must have been on its way to Tacloban. I hastily got dressed and packed my meds and iPad in my Dooney tote bag. At a snail's pace, I clambered down the winding staircase, walking lamely and clinching my swollen knee so as not to put weight on it. I joined my family for breakfast; we had fried fish, bananas, potatoes, fried rice, oatmeal, and yogurt and corned beef sautéed in onion. The breakfast was like a feast. I think Vilma must have served almost everything we bought the day before, seeming like the last supper. This time, the breakfast hit bottom, a menagerie of winged insects seemed to flutter in my stomach. I prayed to God not to let it be like the storm surge of Katrina in New Orleans, those who projected the most horrible and those who contemplated it could not happen. As the Typhoon Haiyan neared Tacloban—one of the hardest hit cities during the storm—the sky was getting darker, and the wind was picking up.

After breakfast I helped Vilma clear the breakfast table; my thoughts made more sense to me now. I hardly had a minute to think about this latest nightmare. It was too late to call Tim. Unfortunately the TV was already off. Outside our windows, which were curtained with gauzy materials, I could see the wind was picking up much harder. My mind was already focused on the storm. Everyone in the house was now very concerned. I could see it in their eyes, even with Betty and Boy.

This time it was obvious that the tempest was not like any other than before. Kasoy, Vilma, and JR started plugging the air conditioner gaps with

Styrofoam to prevent the wind from coming in, and it was strange. I was perplexed. The help was running around to hold the house down. Water was flowing into the house from all over. I walked upstairs to find a place where I can be out of harm's way to videotape the storm and be safe for the coming high waves.

I sat and watched the storm surge from the second floor of the house as it got closer to Tacloban, videotaping with my iPad at around 5:00 A.M. At first, I saw the strange, gray cloud over the city coming toward us. I knew it was about two stories high from the second floor where I was taping. It was like a thick smoke and as it got closer, then it turned into pitch darkness. In that early morning light, the entire city disappeared. My iPad went blank.

Waltzing with the elements, a gust of water suddenly filled the terrace and seeped beneath the glass door where I was taping. With a sudden bolt I realized it was not a gray cloud, but a gigantic wave coming our way. It was so wide I did not know where it started. It seemed to stretch endlessly across the horizon. The storm was raging furiously, more and more violent 315 km winds shrieked through the city for hours, tearing rooftops, shattering windows, hurling appliance out to one side of the house. Furniture and collectibles were flying in all directions.

The tile roof was collapsing. The heavy, steel Iron Gate toppled into two, broken loose from the concrete post. Trees around the house with beautiful orchid blooms, a collection of shrubs, were thrown all over, flowerpots and lampposts smashed by the strong winds. Houses and businesses that have withstood typhoons for decades succumbed to Haiyan. Falling trees ripped down power poles and power lines. It was the scariest four hours; I have never faced a storm like it growing up in Samar.

Still, I was calm, even after I saw the magnitude of the typhoon; I put my iPad next to my tote bag and ran downstairs to get some help, my aching sprained knee felt numb. As I turned around, thinking I should get my iPad and Dooney tote bag, the glass sliding door by the staircase blustered up. Suddenly the glass door exploded and spread shards of glass on the floor where I had been videotaping the storm just a few seconds before. wherever I seemed about to take a step, a new explosion would send me tumbling over. In a single second, I was waltzing from falling fragments and soaring objects.

I was wrestling in the pandemonium, struggling to escape from the scaffolding of porcelain caving in on me. When I reached the first floor, the tile-ceilinged roof by the staircase start crashing down, the six-foot tall porcelain vase at the top of the staircase came tumbling towards me like a bowling ball trying to hit a strike. As I ran across the receiving room, more glass windows were blowing up from all directions. In this extremely large house, it was the scariest experience of my being. I was so blessed to get away alive.

Downstairs, I found myself all alone. My discomfort was great. A twinge of fear went through me like a tidal wave over my head. My heart hardly skips a beat, but in that moment I began to feel I was condemned. Then I began to quaver, seized by a brief spasm of panic; my thoughts were draining out of me. Crashing noises, strong winds were blocking my impulses. I could hardly feel my heart beat as though it had stopped beating; this was the end of me.

No one was around; Betty, her husband Boy, son PJ, and Vilma, the family servant, the driver, JR, and Kasoy, the houseboy, were already hiding, hopefully in a safe place. Forget the iPad, forget everything. Find sanctuary. Moreover, I finally felt my strength and prevailed over my trepidation. The guest bathroom downstairs, I thought in horror, might be safe from the wind, but with the surge, there was no way to swim out. I was all alone and trapped.

I bolted to the guest bathroom, and to my enduring bliss, I found the driver, JR, and the houseboy, Kasoy, who was in his sixties. I was glad to see them. There was nothing to say. I could not collect my thoughts, the rudimentary notions of memory and fragments of thoughts, but was glad for being safe and not being alone. I sat on the toilet and listened to the howling winds, more glass windows crashed, and a wall of water burst through the home. We were unable to do anything against the furious outpouring of the elements.

I sat in the bathroom wrapped up in my own thoughts. I wanted to go back upstairs to find a safe haven, but the shattering, flying glass objects were like being exorcised, the wind like throwing glass rubble in the air, and I could have been the target. The heavy, teak guest furniture was sliding back and forth like someone was rearranging and not sure where to put it.

My crazy thoughts were taking over; I had to stop and focus on wonderful thoughts about my family.

There was no way out from the surging ocean water that was coming. The tsunami felt as if the storm surge would flush us out to the sea. My insides felt as if they were crushed in a terrible weight; I simply listened and sat still. I relived my whole life and in my mind's eye, saw all those dear faces of my husband, Tim, and my three sons, Brian, Ian, AJ, the poor people living in shanty homes, and the places I would certainly never see again. Was it God's plan that I should visit my children on my way to the Philippines? Concerning the hours confined in the bathroom, I had nothing to say. I was resigned to my fate, just thinking I was at the mercy of fate.

Tim
Our worried family's conversation in U.S. and Doha Qatar.
November 9, 2013, Saturday: I woke up, made a pot of coffee, and turned on the TV. Nothing new on TV since last night, so I headed to the computer. There were reports and photos showing the destruction and death. I was now feeling worried and lost, because I did not know what to do.

I then went to twitter, started to follow the feed #Yolanda, and watched that for a little bit. There was a Tweet about reporting missing persons, so I went to the link and Google had started a site to report missing persons. I reported both Emy and Betty as missing. I also found a website for The Red Cross, Philippines, and posted Emy and Betty as missing with them as well.

I was not surprised by the lack of coverage, because all communication lines had been severely damaged, and most power lines were now on the ground. The Tacloban Airport had been destroyed, so no one could get in or out of the city.

Betty's house was well-built, and I would have felt somewhat comforted if I had known Emy and the family were in that house during Yolanda's devastating trip through town. That was probably some wishful thinking on my part, as it also would not have surprised me if the 250 mph winds had left it in rubble.

7:01 A.M.	Tim's Facebook post
	Photos out of Tacloban are showing much destruction. People are out but no news from the family or friends.
10:01 A.M.	Brian's Facebook post
	Tacloban City is flat, and thousands are in trouble. There is almost no news coverage here. It is not on the news agenda. Just meaningless shit been reported... I am still waiting to hear from mom and family...hate this.
11:19 A.M.	Kristina's Facebook post
	TACLOBAN, my hometown, I pray for you, to all of my loved ones, STAND up and PRAY for a better tomorrow...have faith...God is merciful...
12:44 P.M.	Messenger: Tim, Sandy, and Kristina
	Tim: Hi again. The day before the typhoon, I talked with Emy. She said they were going to stay at your Mom's home. Do you know if that is where they were? Is there a "safe" room? Stay positive
Sandy:	When I talked with mom, she was at home, Uncle Tim. Network signals may be possible by tomorrow. Nevertheless, I am afraid that they may have run out of batteries already. Nevertheless, I am constantly trying to reach them.
Tim:	Sandy thanks for the update.

Sometime Saturday afternoon, Erlinda called and said they contacted the U.S. Embassy website in Manila, and I should do the same. I went to their website, left a message about Emy being in Tacloban, and asked them to notify me if they received any news. I got a "canned" message back, listing twenty links for all types of issues, so I figured that was not useful. A day later, I did get a response from someone saying they would notify me if the learned of their whereabouts.

Emy

November 8, 2013: Tacloban, four hours after Haiyan's wrath. All my self-consciousness is back, and I am in a state of shock. In addition, I am dreadfully terrified, but I am going to walk tall with strength and resiliency. Air and water are the main elements of life, but this was truly the opposite. I braced for what I knew was going to be a disaster. Typhoon Haiyan was physically, the most brutal and overwhelming experience; it was too loud to hear anything else. I felt like I was going to fade, thought it was the end of it. It was the longest four hours I have endured.

I do not know how to convey the horrifying and terrifying violence of the catastrophe. I did not think the house was going to withstand the wrath of Haiyan. With a bit of luck, a phenomenon, the three-story high waves did not reach the house or neighborhood, but the horrendous 315-km wind was inexorable.

As the typhoon slowly calmed down, I was still in a state of shock. We started cleaning up the debris. The Christmas garlands that had been put out a few days before were all blown around, beautiful draperies were torn, everything was immersed, drenched. I helped sweep up the water, for it was flooding the house. It must have rained all day. We rolled out some of the Egyptian rugs we'd stored prior to the super storm surge of Haiyan and some breakable items. The rest of what was left standing was history.

By late afternoon, the storm miraculously had passed. But the horror of Haiyan sank in I pinched myself. I walked upstairs and my sprained knee was back to nag me. I saw the destruction of the city that had been humming with life just hours before. Nothing was left. Everything was flattened. What was left of Tacloban seemed like a fine steam rising from the ground, like low-lying fog coming from the ocean on an early morning.

I could see the whole city in all directions of the horizon. From our terrace, a haze and misty fog with a sort of ash color steamed over the horizon. It looked as though the city was blown off the surface of earth and carried out to sea by the surge and the strong winds of Haiyan. I felt like we were the ones that had survived. I saw my iPad under a table twenty feet across from where I had left it, my black and pink Dooney tote dangling from the terrace railing, and Betty's collection of figurines vases blown to pieces. The corner guest rooms where a former Philippine president and some dignitaries stayed were all windblown, the glass windows on both corners were gone, in pieces, the four bedposts and canopy toppled by the falling tile roof.

Some objects seemed to have lifted with miraculously benign force; therefore, so it was that a room air conditioner attached to a window was lifted out by the wind and deposited in its original shape over the house and down to the poolside. Wherein almost everything around the house was in shambles, disarray, the ceiling-to-floor glass windows were shattered into pieces, and the metal doorframes were bent. It was total madness.

Repercussions. Outside the street below, the image was blurred. Gigantic mango trees were uprooted as if radishes, power poles and wires that had been dangling before the storm, now were almost ropes wrapped around the posts. Homes were roofless, only the structures were left standing. It looked like a ghost town, no community, no nothing and almost no life, except us. Everything was left in a rubble and wind blown.

I was able to see the distraction from miles away. The high-pressure regions over the Pacific sent the storm surge past a gap in the eastern end of Samar into a corridor 112 km wide, through which it rushed to Tacloban in a strangled buffeting that scraped the surface of everything in its path. The sole vegetation visible was barren, looking like the after effect of a forest fire.

On the houses that the storm surge left standing was a residue of stony gravel. There rose a chain of prow-shaped, saw-tooth, razor-edged mountains stripped by the elements down to the bare rocks. Coconut trees looked like match sticks. All day we remained, clearing the water out; it was raining torrentially.

I kept off my nervousness by clearing the debris around the house. Ghostly silence, stillness, the amount of devastation was enormous. It was absolutely eerie. My anxiety increased. Certainly the most devastating blow was for those people living around the coastal areas; I hoped they made it to safety. The crying and howling dogs from the day before were now quiet. I hoped they were okay. We were alone.

I spent the rest of the day helping remove water from my cousin's home and picking up the family's scattered belongings, sorting some memorabilia that could be salvaged; the clear, blue water in the swimming pool now was black. We used it to flush the toilet.

An average of twenty typhoons hit the Philippines every year. In 2011, typhoons killed 1,200 people, displaced 300,000 and destroyed more than 10,000 homes. Nevertheless, this one could reach 10,000 or more dead.

Evening of November 8, 2013: Tacloban, the darkness of Haiyan. All communication, water, and electricity were down. We did nothing but try to salvage what was left after a solemn dinner of rice, fish, fried chicken, fish soup, and fruit, Vilma the family servant and I started scouting for a dry place to sleep before nightfall. A small office with a low ceiling above the garage and the servants' quarters were a blessing. It had a narrow steep stairway leading to the kitchen and to the main house restroom with a locked iron grill from the outside.

I slept on a partially wet cushion on a hard floor. I rested in the dark with my eyes closed, feeling predestined with nowhere else to escape from the mystery of sheer darkness. I was afraid to open my eyes; I had the feeling of being in an endless pit with no way out. Getting my pulse up, I tried to overcome today's tempest and the stillness of the night. I must have been tired from clearing the debris, and after a numbing glass of brandy, I somewhat slept well.

November 9, 2013: Hazy and cloudy with some drizzle, I awakened mortified and furious. I did a yoga child pose, slowly listening to my body as to which way to move. I heard my bones making a squeaky sound as I moved to roll face down into dog pose and used the force of my upper body to stir up. Going down the steep stairwell was hard, as I hung to the railing, making one step at a time, my whole being was throbbing, my right knee swollen.

Gloomy morning and everyone was at the breakfast table. We had leftovers for breakfast, and it seemed like no one felt hungry. We sat at the breakfast table as though something were stuck in our throats. We were all in awe. After clearing the table, I left Vilma. I sat at the patio, nursing a cup of coffee after a long, sleepless night. I found out, JR, our driver had to go home on foot to Santa Rita to visit his young wife Marissa Cajefe and four young children, ranging from four years old to a newborn. I felt bad that he could not be with his family at this time of disaster. For personal reasons, I did not want him to go. He was the only strong person in the house, physically strong and unswerving. He walked from V & G subdivision to Santa Rita, Samar about 37 miles and walked back the next day. I begged him to come back right away, as soon as he found out his family was all right.

By late afternoon, I saw a lone helicopter hovering up high like it was afraid to come closer. It made two rounds and was gone on the horizon. I desperately waved a torn drapery, and I felt reassured that someone found us. We were not alone. I had pictured myself being on an uninhabited island with nowhere to go, and we were the only ones. I prayed to God that he saw me waving; dear God make him come back.

Down on the street below, I saw a few people walking by with bags full of new clothing. And someone was also hauling a rolling cart, something a store would use to hang clothes for display. I wondered where it was coming from, these people were casually walking, carrying goods? How could anyone be in that condition in time of crisis? I found out they were looters from a nearby shopping mall. Robinsons was looted. The security guards surrendered to the mob of looters barging into the mall when a limited distribution broke down into chaos.

Tacloban was filled with despair at the soaring death toll; people are now becoming desperate for food. Some took what they need. Some took what they want. There were reports of shootings. My lord, this is not going to be good. I watched these people carting goods from the terrace of the house. Three men were already camping out at one end of Betty's property. I asked Vilma to see if she knew them, and immediately she went to Barangay Capitan house to report it, to make them move out, since they don't live in the neighborhood.

There was no one in command after the storm, which sparked more fear of vagaries, as though it were the end of the world. Other survivors were getting aggressive as they took advantage of the whole situation, wherein some of them must be starving with nothing to eat and no food supply. I sympathized with them.

For my part, I kept full of activity, cleaning out some remains of broken glass and collecting drenched draperies and clothes. It rained heavily, sporadically, the whole day so that we can barely maintain to put a stop the already flooded house. However, it helped get my mind off what would happen next. I heard there was another typhoon named Zorayda looming over Pacific Ocean, but we managed to have missed it, thank God.

I wanted to go out after I heard rumors that a cargo plane had been transporting relief goods into the city and taking refugees out, but I didn't know where or how to get there. The roads were all buried with rubble, trees, power poles, and power lines. There was not any communication from local authorities, so we rely on rumors. I was apprehensive to get out; I had to know what is out there. If I were to go, I wouldn't even have the slightest thought as to where.

Beyond comprehension, the local government, unprepared for this disaster, was nowhere to be found. President Benigno Aquino III, who traveled by helicopter to Tacloban on Sunday, the third day after the typhoon, did not seem to have a sound plan of action and was unaware of just how bad things were in Tacloban and elsewhere—how many people were stranded or missing, or needed a place to stay or how much food, water, and aid was needed. Almost certainly, it had to do with Anderson Cooper's being in town that he attempted to visit.

The president said that his government had deployed several hundred soldiers "to show the strength of the state and deter looting," according to his *official* website, which wasn't accurate. I saw three soldiers on our drive out to Samar. Haiyan had left in her wake what was Anderson Cooper had called a "total disaster zone," where people were getting desperate.

The Philippine president should have had declared the state of calamity after seeing the horrible devastation. That could have hastened the delivery of aid from various international groups and some Filipino communities abroad. "The need is massive; the need is immediate; and you can't reach everyone," Interior Secretary Roxas said. Five days later, the authorities were still struggling to meet their immediate needs. Local and national government lacked the capability, especially in an already poor country.

We still had yet to see the worldwide aid; the effort through government distribution system was not enough. Overwhelmed authorities admitted they were unable to get relief supplies to Tacloban. Although some were handing out small packets to each household, one little packet is not enough for a household of six. None of the imported relief goods were in the ration bags except for some local and expired canned goods. For five days, we were in Tacloban, and we did not get any relief, although we did not need it for now.

Typhoon Haiyan threatened to become the deadliest disaster in Philippine history, surpassing Tropical Storm Thelma, which killed 5,000 people in 1991. With sustained wind speeds of 150 to 170 mph, Haiyan is among the strongest storms on record. (According to ABS/CBN TV Patrol Tacloban 87 days after the storm surge, the death toll was more than 20,000.)

Tacloban was destroyed; some people are losing their minds from hunger or from losing their families. People are becoming violent. Some broke into shops that had withstood the typhoon by hammering through glass windows and wrenching open steel doors. They are looting business establishments and the malls just to find food. I am afraid in my vivid thoughts that in one week, people will be killing from hunger.

Misinformation. The latest Philippine government estimates suggested that 9.5 million people—about ten percent of the country—were affected by the storm surge that took place, with more than 600,000 displaced from their homes. Many roads remained impassable, according to the U.N. office responsible for humanitarian affairs. Some of the injured had no access to medical care. Even in Tacloban, one of the first areas accessed by aid workers, it took six hours to make the fourteen-mile round trip between the airport and the city because of the damage, officials said. There were five hospitals but not all were operable due to the storm surge.

During John Kerry's visit, he listened to a flurry of briefings and asked questions about the recovery:

"Who is making the birds reconstruction plan?" Kerry asked.

"The National Economic and Development Authority," he was told.

"How many hospitals are operating?" Kerry asked.

"Fifteen in Tacloban," they told him.

"What about the junk on the roads?" Kerry asked.

"There are several landfills," Ben Hemmingway, a regional advisor for the U.S. Agency for International Development, told him. "They leave it out there for several days, let it grow, and it is picked away for scrap metal and other items that can be repurposed. Then it goes across a bridge,"

The only bridge I know is San Juanico bridge to Samar. Are they using Samar as the garbage dump? Please do not let it be.

Foreign volunteers must rely on what information and direction they get from the national and local governments. Answering John Kerry's question about operating hospitals, there were eight (and some non-operable), namely Remedios Trinidad, Romualdez Med Center, Holy Virgin, Tacloban Doctors Saint Paul, Bethany, Eastern Visayas Regional Medical Center, and the Provincial Hospital, which was not even in Tacloban. It was in Candahug, Palo, Leyte. According to a reliable source, Attorney Leslie Adolfo, most of the hospitals mentioned were non-operable after the storm surge.

"It is vital that we reach those who are stranded in isolated areas as they are at risk of further threats such as malnutrition and exposure to bad weather," the Red Cross (ICRC) said. The agency had been receiving reports that some gunmen were roaming around, putting relief operations to affected residents in the area at risk. To this date, the local, unitary government is hampering and slowing down the relief distribution. For one thing, many had nowhere to go. Supplies had been limited to begin with and slow for some of the refugees from the storm. City leaders had no real plan for anyone else. Meanwhile, it was impossible to leave Tacloban. The majority of them are poor people without cars or any place to go.

At last, the actual aid disembarked from air, land, and sea. The United States of America (Thanks to Mr. Anderson Cooper for your gallant statement!) and the whole worlds drew closer to the rescue. U.S. Navy helicopters flew sorties from the aircraft carrier USS *George Washington* off the coast, dropping water and food to isolated communities.

The U.S. military said it would send about 1,000 more troops, along with additional ships and aircrafts to join the aid effort. So far, the U.S. military has moved 190 tons of supplies and flown nearly 200 sorties. The focus of the aid effort is on providing life-saving aid for those who survived. The search for missing people is lower in the government's priorities

According to the head of the country's disaster management agency, Eduardo del Rosario, the coast guard, the navy, and civilian volunteers are searching the sea for the dead and the missing. After the preliminary days of pandemonium when no aid reached the people without roofs over their heads, an international aid effort was gathering steam.

"We are starting to see the turning of the corner!" said John Ging, a top U.N. humanitarian official in New York. He said 107,500 people have received food assistance so far, and 11 foreign and 22 domestic medical teams are in operation. The U.S. arrived and brought all relief supplies directly to the devastated areas, where the people were starving to death.

I read in the Manila Bulletin that supplies were stuck in Manila, starting at the customs with sorting donated boxes from non-donation. Although planes begun arriving with badly needed supplies, much of the aid remained undistributed because of government bureaucrats and impassable roads, cluttered by debris from broken buildings.

To make things worse, Philippine president, Benigno Aquino, had sanctioned the temporary release of the city's prisoners during his first visit to Tacloban. Poor Judgment. The first day the prisoners were out, there were reports of rapes at the downtown area. Oh Lord, this was going to get bad. With renewed heavy rain showers and deteriorating security, police failed to report for duty—armed gunmen and looting have been reported, making matter shoddier for an already exhausted population without shelter, food, or potable water.

There was one C-130 bringing in relief foods and taking back some evacuees to Manila and Cebu. There was a report that one of the family members of the city's mayor was missing from their seaside resort of Barangay San Jose. Popularly known as the "Astrodome" was a five-thousand-seat indoor arena for basketball tourneys, other sporting activities, concerts, and other big gatherings like the Search for Ms. Tacloban. It also housed multiple bars and businesses and was severely damaged due to Typhoon Haiyan. It served as evacuation center.

Mothers with young children and older people were advised to evacuate to the Astrodome. The signal #4 storm surge forewarning was not as decisive as they thought. Luckily, it withstood the typhoon; thousands of people have gathered there and many have died.

Guiaun was actually where Haiyan first made landfall, and it was crushed. The shoreline from Tacloban to Ormoc was demolished by the storm surge, washed out or devastated. Dead bodies were under the debris along the shoreline. I began to panic; my world was standing as still as I was. Relief goods were not reaching us, but my main concern was to leave Tacloban. We must get out of here and seek refuge somewhere. All power was cut off, so we had to depend on hearsay.

I had to think about the best way to get away. I was so worried I could barely eat. Our foods, water, candles, cooking gas were getting near to the ground. Friends of the family were coming, asking for food. They had been walking for hours. One family friend, his name was Raymond, walked with two young children for five hours to Betty's house to ask for food. Raymond had many horror stories to tell from his way to Betty's home. People were walking with wounds and limping. I had had enough.

Tim in South Dakota

Saturday was when I received a call from Gladys, Emy's cousin. These two have had a special bond through the years, and Gladys wanted to know what I knew at this point. I did not have much to tell her, but we would talk and text daily until Emy was in California.

6:58 P.M.   Tim's message to Emy
              Darling many people are very worried about you all. You went home during the WORST storm EVER. Pictures look bad but I know you are OK. Communications to be restore in a few days. Love you

8:16 P.M.   Tim's Facebook post
              Authorities are predicting the loss of life could reach 10,000 in Tacloban, Leyte, Philippines. Few structures left standing within a kilometer of the shore. I cannot comprehend what that day was like. It seems like all I was doing was watching TV, surfing the Internet, or talking to someone. Brian, Ian, and AJ were having a harder time than I knew. The lack of information was tearing them apart inside. Another late night before I went to bed, said my prayers, and prayed for sleep.

Emy

November 10, 2013: Tacloban was in darkness. No food. No electricity. The entire Tacloban city was in sheer darkness, a new beginning of time. Memories of yesterday were lost. My families' third candlelit dinner was quiet; Vilma served rice, fish, and vegetables. After a solemn dinner, Betty, Boy, and PJ went to bed.

That evening I had to assess what I should do with my project in Hinangutdan. I had to assume that Tacloban would not recover as everyone thought. I had to go home to the U.S. and come back on a later date to finish my project. My thoughts were weighing my whole being. As I gazed at Vilma clearing the dishes, I poured brandy to drown my sorrow. For some reason before the storm, I had bought two bottles of French brandy that I thought had been wine.

That night was one of complete darkness, without a gleam of light but the flickering candle. I sat alone wrapped in obscurity, having a sip of brandy, lost as I was in my thoughts as though the external world had ceased to exist. I saw a flickering light like a miniature star giving off a glow—a mysterious, wearied light. A lone firefly was tapping on the glass window that had been left unbroken by the super typhoon. It appeared to pacify my emotion of incomprehension, unsure of what motivation was there for tomorrow. I accepted as true that angels were watching us; that everything would be well. It was eerily quiet and seemed cold; I must be silent and get pleasure from the companionship of a firefly while waiting for Vilma to join me. After two glasses of brandy, my new firefly friend helped me break away from the heartache for all the people that had perished, the homeless, and the lucky ones that lived to tell the tale and endure the struggle for survival. For some miracle, we were spared by the super typhoon.

I was also fortunate to have Vilma, the family servant, who was so kind to be present during my wretchedness. After she finished her never-ending chores, she heated a gallon can of water and mixed with cold in washtub. I bathed in the warm water, which helped soothe my throbbing body and soul. In addition, Vilma retrieved a partially soaked bed cushion. She smoothed and dried a place for me to sleep on the floor. It was rigid for my knees to get up and down.

After wrenching my right knee from the boating mishap the few days prior to Haiyan, combined with not getting any younger, my squeaky knees were a predicament in this new escapade. As I lay in darkness on the thin mattress, watching the flickering candlelight, I started to feel relaxed and was about to sleep. I heard gunshots echoing from a nearby neighborhood. I was overwrought; my days of paralysis hit me. Being here holed up with nowhere to run was nothing more than a devastating bluster. After a long, wakeful night, I got up and walked around without direction in the darkness. I was hearing noises of someone on foot upstairs. I must be imagining it. I saw a flashlight from outside and heard motorcycles humming, I was horrified.

Early that morning, feeling weary, exhaustion was setting in. The gunshots we heard were from a family home that was looted by prisoners (that the Philippine sanction to freedom). His wife was raped, and they killed them all. Lethargy sank in. I felt so helpless for all of us; the night of complete darkness dulled my spirit. I was beginning to be psychologically shattered. I tried to read old partially wet newspapers to help nourish my psyche. It is hard to describe the actions that I am trying to put into words, for myself to experience it.

Tim

November 10, 2013: The TV and Internet were showing so much destruction and death. The pictures and videos were unbelievable and saddening. How could anyone survive this? I still had not heard from Emy after four days or so, but I tried to stay positive and had to believe they were alive. How long could they survive? Food and water were scarce, and looters were stealing to survive. I knew communications were still down, but hope was on the way.

8:52 A.M.   Tim's Facebook post
                According to the Philippine Daily Inquirer, communications are beginning to be restored in parts of Tacloban, but

	the lack of a power system is still a problem. I am still praying for all the folks in the Philippines.
8:55 A.M.	Messenger: Tim, Brian, Ian, AJ, Sandy, and Kristina
	Tim: I am happy some of your friends are receiving news from the Philippines. Do any of them live near Tacloban? Have you heard from Garrett?
	Tim: I have emailed the Philippine Red Cross, asking for some information and filed two missing person forms. We will have to wait some more. Hang in there. I love you all
Sandy:	Garret is in Manila right now, Uncle Tim. He asked one of our cousins who were scheduled to board the C-130 plane for Tacloban to check the situation at V&G once he is there. He will pass by our house, and I hope we will get some news soon. Garret plans to go there and travel by land.
Tim:	I am happy to hear that. Tell Garret to be safe.
Sandy:	Will do Uncle Tim. He is getting info first from our cousin to assess the situation there and make his move.
Ian:	Let me know, hope all is well
Tim:	I sent an email to the U.S. Embassy in Manila and gave them Betty's address; see what happens.
2:26 P.M.	Messenger: Tim and Sheryl
Tim:	Hi Sheryl, I just saw your Facebook post. Is everyone ok? Where are they now?
	Sheryl: I have not talked to them firsthand yet. It is fortunate that my cousin was able to call Aunt Cecilia and had a brief conversation with her (less than 30seconds only). However, glad to know they are ok in v and g. Nevertheless, the house is damage...
Tim:	Thank you for the news. Is Emy with them?
Sheryl:	I am not sure. I do not know who is with them right now... I'll keep in touch once I'm able to reach them. Try calling this number, Uncle Tim. This is the number that they were able to call
Tim:	Sheryl would you verify the number please. Seems too long

Sheryl:　　　　　That is a cell phone number.

Emy

November 11, 2013: Dark and cloudy. Today is my oldest son Brian's birthday. Happy Birthday Son. I felt a spasm of anguish for him, and it hurt. A new kind of loneliness was setting in as I sat in this eerie environment with flicker-flashes of mostly dark thoughts. I did not think I would ever be with my family again. I told myself that I was not going to make it home alive.

I could hardly swallow my breakfast; it felt like my heart was blocking my throat. Good thing we had a stock of bananas; it would give me energy to think and find a way to get out of Tacloban. Today I realized my family must be worried sick about me. I miss my husband, Tim, more than anything at this moment; I needed his big hugs right now. I remember Tim telling me to leave Tacloban as soon as I could early on Thursday November 7, the day before the super storm Haiyan made landfall.

My husband, Tim, gave me the license to share the hard truths in life, always ready to understand my outbursts. My being missing for four days must be killing his nurturing side. He would trivialize my outbursts with a practical saneness as befits a pragmatic man who favors semantics. We had been blissfully happy after our second marriage, and I miss him so much. Our children were even happier.

I felt so cold and weak at just the thought of my family not knowing where I might be. I grieved the death, the illusions of my own death. I was feeling ill inside could not sleep at all; I was so powerless. I felt like I was going to lose my mind if we stayed in this place any longer. I was sure my family was watching the news and imagining crazy things. I feared for my life and my cousin, Betty, and her husband, Menandro, was also frail and could barely walk.

We were in the middle of this city with no way out; it looked like a jagged terrain and unfathomable jungle, uprooted trees, power lines like vines, and power poles blocking the whole neighborhood. We have lived to tell the tale from the storm surge, were lucky that the two-story waves did not reach the house, but the 315-km winds did. The house withstood the colossal winds except for the glass windows and part of the cement and tile roof. However, were we going to continue to exist from the other elements—looters looting for survival and prisoners that were sanctioned by the president? Still no sign of the local government. The Barangay Capitan did nothing for her community; there was no news bulletin on how to cope with this disaster. She had no reports to tell us of where to get the relief food, of a call center for the families in agony. The unknown frightened me; I could hold on. I felt my heart stop and start to beat faster.

I sat at the secret garden surrounded by rubble and debris. I closed my eyes to rest my head and listened to my heart as it pounded slowly. I prayed for someone from Hinangutdan to come and see me. My fear of unknown horrors was playing with my head. Friends of my cousin Betty were stopping over, asking for food and some clothing. We had bananas to share and some clothing; they looked doomed and had some dreadful stories to tell from their long walk. I had to keep my mind off of it and read something to keep my memory intact. I did not want to listen any longer, for it was making me miserable. I walked upstairs to look out for miracles. From above, I saw neighbors covering their roofs with plastic canopies, some were drying clothes on a string line and washing clothes from well water, and others were packing and moving out.

Everyone seemed busy. As for me, I knew I had to leave the island or get out of the house; it was like being a prisoner of your own home. I wanted to venture out and see what were my chances of getting out, but how, where? I did not have a map of the city and chances are I would be lost or die in fear. PJ, Betty's son, got back from his motorcycle ride and told us that a helicopter was charging P10,000 per passenger for those who wanted to get out of town.

After Vilma cleaned up the breakfast table and prepared for lunch, I asked Betty if Vilma, the family servant, could come along with me to the airport and see if the rumors were true. I was so relieved, knowing we would be able to get away. Later I found out that poor kid lied to me. There was not any private helicopter at all.

It had been dismal and drizzly for days after Haiyan. Today the sky was blue, a hard, blue sky that shone over the threadbare mountains and desolate city, which flashed in the sunlight.

Tim

Sheryl:	Another storm is coming name Zorayda. I hope it does not hit Tacloban. They had enough.
Tim:	Another storm would be terrible. No connection to the cell phone number yet. Will keep trying.
Sheryl:	Yes Uncle Tim, there are only few selected areas with cell phone signals. I hope it gets better in the coming days. Are you planning to go there?
Tim:	I am thinking of options. I am not sure what to do.
Sheryl:	Same here Uncle Tim. No flights are going there. Only a C-130 plane where relief goods are loaded. This plane also evacuates people in Tacloban. However, you have to go into the needle, Long waits and Long line.
Tim:	Maybe they can evacuated to Manila.
Sheryl:	By land also you have to walk from San Juanico going to the respective places in Leyte, Only motorcycle or on foot. It is possible but they have to register. Nevertheless, they are too many. You can rent a chartered plane (correct me if I'm wrong, it's a 6-seater plane).
Tim:	I guess we need to continue praying for their safety
Sheryl:	My sister-in-law has considered this option, but it would be last resort as it cost much. They want to evacuate my hubby's family. But*
Tim:	I think the airport will open in a couple days
Sheryl:	Yes, but fully booked.

3:22 P.M.	Tim's message to Emy
	Darling I have been talking with your sister Erlinda. She loves you as we all do. Sheryl posted you might be at another house as Betty's was damaged. We are Praying for you all. Love you
4:58 P.M.	AJ's Facebook post
	Be safe Emy Cajipe-Matthews n Robbie along w the rest

of my family and friends in the Philippines.

7:51 P.M.   Brian's Facebook post
                 Moms good, she is in Santa Rita a town about 45 min boat
                 rides from Tacloban lol! Good stuff.

I was getting ready for bed when I saw Brian's message. I got up and had to follow this news. It was confusing, a little misleading, but we started to learn Emy, and the family was okay. Brian's Facebook post and message indicated Emy was in Santa Rita and this confused me. While I was hoping it to be true, I needed to know for sure. (Actually, she was still in Tacloban. Garret's post was a little cryptic and confusing.)

8:45 P.M.   Messenger: Tim and Brian
                 Brian: Mom is fine! Did you see Garrets post?
                 Tim: Wonderful news thank you. I did not see his post
                 would you please share it?
                 Brian: sharing.

Emy

Audacious saunter: Vilma and I meandered down Mango Street. The blue sky glittered like a new-honed knife, accompanying the physical exertion of the sun. On our way, it was like through ruthless situation, like skip, hop, jump over a puddle, dirty ditch, duck under the power lines, swamp-covered trees, power poles, and galvanized roofs. I tried not to look to the marshy area and the side of the road, as you would see everything from dead bodies to sandals. After three turns to the left, we reached Maharlika highway, this one was even worse to attempt to walk, concrete power poles and tangled up power lines were massive as we tried to make our way.

Vilma and I walked for four hours. Vilma was twenty years younger and had scoliosis and asthma as Betty reminded me later. I forgot about her weakness as we kept on walking to the nearest and only airport in Tacloban, attempting to board the only cargo plane that had begun evacuating the island residents once a day. They would bring relief in the morning and evacuate people in the afternoon.

A city with population of millions, but they only had one transport plane. Only a few people were getting relief and no one knew where to get the aid. Everything was word of mouth. There was no communication: the mayor of Tacloban's local government was nowhere to be found. Even with just a few being spared by the storm surge, they needed to send a leader in each Barangay to coordinate relief efforts. Help was beginning to trickle into the Philippines in the wake of the devastating Super Typhoon Haiyan; however, it is far from enough. Desperation is setting in for the thousands of people with nowhere to go for clean water, food, or medical care.

When a Philippine Air Force C-130 arrived at the typhoon-wrecked airport Tuesday after dawn, people had been camping out, more than 3,000 people hoped to escape the devastation from the storm surge on the tarmac past a broken iron fence. Only a few hundred made it aboard; the rest were shattered. The rain-lashed city was short of food and water and littered with uncounted bodies. Just a dozen soldiers and several police held the crowd back.

Chilling scenario: this is already the fourth day after the typhoon; I approached the immense line to board the planes, people looked tired, in distress. I had the sensation as though I made my escape. A terrible sight, the only clear area was the plane's landing site. The rest all around us was as if a bomb had been dropped and everything was toppled bodies and debris on top of each other. I covered my face and gasped my breath: there was a lifeless woman in a birthing position covered with cardboard who had halfway given birth to her child in the street curb. I felt a chill shoot from the back of my neck all the way down my spine.

I had never seen anything like it; my heart was clanging in my chest like a fire alarm. I was panting, perspiring heavily under the scorching sun. Had this really happened? I could not look any farther. The scene made me turn back home and beseech my cousin for us to abscond immediately. That was four days after the storm; bodies still were not being collected. No one was around to take care of them. Other citizens were out looking in hopelessness for their loved ones.

I thought to myself what is next? These dead bodies are going to decompose, if no one collects them. I saw dead bodies decomposing under the sun, distended corpses lying face down in the muddy rubble covered with boards or blown out fragments. Walking along the Maharlika highway was a debacle, nothing like it was four days earlier with jeepneys, cars, and tricycles; pedicabs honking and beeping, people waiting for rides. It had been full of life.

Now it was wholly a town of the living dead. Nobody knew where to go. A family with young children were picking odds and ends to build an improvised shelter before nightfall, cooking food along the highway, pitching water at the dirty canal. It was a horrendous panorama for me or for anyone to have experienced such a complete disaster.

According to the latest figures by the Philippines's main disaster agency, 6,000 people died and 12,487 were injured. I think the government was trying to keep the death toll under ten thousand in order to keep the relief money away from United Nations. Many of the bodies remained tangled among piles of debris or lining the road in body bags that seeped fetid liquid. Some are believed to have been swept out to sea.

Vilma and I approached home and I saw Betty, the Barangay Captain, and friends sitting along the street curb. I did not quite understand them. Vilma and I went inside the house, tired physically and mentally exhausted and thirsty because we forgot to bring water. With the heat and the horror we saw along the way, I had to sit down and recover from the horrific scene from our four-hour walk. Vilma poured us glasses of thirst-quenching warm Coke. I gave her some money before the typhoon, and she stocked up on Coke, which she enjoyed immensely.

After a short rest I looked for Betty's husband to tell him privately what I saw. Betty, on the other hand, was not about to leave. I could see it in the way she gathered things around the house. She felt that this would be restored in few days. I admired her resiliency and I do respect her. I told Boy that we had to leave, for health reasons and for everybody's sake. "You may not know it, but in another day or two there will be a pandemic, and it is going to be anarchy," I said.

I could not describe the most brutal catastrophe and devastating repulsion that was left by the storm surge of Haiyan. There was not any law or order at all. I saw a long line of people carrying containers and groups of men punching a hole to a gas tank in what use to be a gasoline station. It was like scooping out the gas from a well. People walked like zombies, some carrying sacks full of rice from a flooded warehouse, some just sitting along the road in astonishment, thinking what they were going to do next or what would happen to them and their loved ones.

Some are looking for their relatives. Mass departures of people went in different directions; it was a horrifying experience. My heart started to ache and I felt like I would be sick. The air was so full of rubble dust that when we came home, we were covered with a thin film of dirt.

Apparently, my family in the U.S. was gathering information of our survival:

        Tim: Where is Garret?

        Brian: Under terrah sepiot

        Tim: Twitter?

        Tim: Sheryl shows them all safe in Tacloban still

8:49 P.M.   Ian's Facebook post

        Mom and family confirmed safe in the PI @Bdub_JJ @AJ_MMA hope all involved get positive news as well!

9:02 P.M.   Tim's Facebook post

        Apparently, Emy Cajipe-Matthews and family are safe and no longer in Tacloban. Thank you all for your support the past several days.

9:18 P.M.   Messenger: Tim, Sheryl, Sandy, and Kristina

        Tim: Brian said he saw a post from Garret and the family is now in Santa Rita. Have you heard from Garret?

        Sheryl: Yes, they are in Santa Rita, Uncle Tim. Just talked to Garrett, we have the same thought that they should ride the C-130. They are having scarcity of food and water right now.

        Tim: Thank you for the good news. I hope they can get out soon.

        Sheryl: I am afraid they will starve if they are not be evacuated to Manila

        Tim: I hope supplies arrive soon

Sandy: Uncle Tim, I just spoken with Garret. They are all safe. They are not in Santa Rita, Samar. They are still in Tacloban. Road is not passable, so transfer is not possible. All are accounted for, Mom, Dad, Aunt Emy, Vilma, Pj and Tita Lina.

Sheryl: We are getting mixed information...Aunt Lina is at Calbiga right now. I have just talked to her via cell phone. In addition, yes, mom, dad, aunt emy, Te VI, and PJ are in V and G. All accounted for. Mel was able to call PJ. He is on his way to Nula-Tula. Highways are clear already and passable in that area. San I talked to PJ.

Sandy: Yes, I did talk to PJ.

Sheryl: San was able to call dad.

Tim: Confusing, but thanks for the updates.

Sheryl: Tito Tim was able to call dad. They will leave for Manila tonight. I am still crying, happy at the same time that I was able to hear his voice.. they will travel by land.

Tim: Wow, I am so happy for you all. Can't believe they can leave.

Sandy: I know the feeling. Glad they are all safe.

Tim: Will they leave tomorrow? That must be a long drive. Is there fuel?

Sheryl: I do not know, Uncle Tim, but I know they will manage.

Tim: Sweet Jesus Son of God, We thank you!

Sandy:Yes Uncle Tim, Our prayers have been answered.

Tim: You are all awesome!

Sheryl: God is good. All praises to Him!

9:19 PM P.M.   Tim's message to Emy

Darling I hear that you are now in Santa Rita. I hope this is true and that all of you are fine.

9:41 P.M.   Garret's Facebook post

I just talk to my Auntie Lina from Sta. Rita. She assured me that my family is a-ok. Dad, Mom, PJ, Tita Emy, JR, and Auntie V were Ok. Damage to the house was huge. Water and food are in badly needed. Tacloban is like a huge funeral house and the smell is unbearable. There is too much looting and no banking service available because they have all been ransacked. People need to walk five hrs just to cross San Juanico depending on your location in the city. People are getting food in Calbiga and Catbalogan. Much has to has to done to restore the vibrant city, BUT I know we can make it. Keep BELIEVING!

11:06 P.M. Tim's message to Emy
     Darling I now hear you are still in Tacloban and might leave for Manila. Please be safe.

At least we knew they were alive and safe. What had they gone through? Did they still have food? Would they be able to leave? I still had many questions and no answers. I went to bed feeling a little relieved, said my prayers, and I think I slept.

Emy

In the Wakeful Hours of Tacloban – Darkness. At the house it was getting late, so I assisted Vilma in preparing our dinner before it got dark. We had to save our candles, cooking gas was also getting low, so she has to use the pogon, a cooking stove made of cement hidden at the back of the house behind the secret patio. We had one more jug of drinking water; I started collecting rainwater for drinking and cooking. Our dinner now was beginning to trickle down to rice and leftover fried chicken and fish.

The night was like any other night after Haiyan—I was not able to sleep. The darkness made me impatient. The scenes from our walk made it even worse. I was getting lightheaded and irrational fears set in. I could not stand being enclosed and felt like the house was shaking. It was so dark at night, like an infinite, sheer darkness. I am going to lose my mind if we stay one more day.

JR, the driver, parked both cars close to one side of the gate that was blown by the strong winds. I helped put tangled wires like a trap and a scrap of galvanized roof to make a noise just in case the looters or prisoners would try to crawl under the SUV. I felt somewhat safe, but what if they climbed out from the tall fence and to the open windows? Many dark demons lurked in my waking mind. We did not have any fortification if the looters and prisoners decided to come and ransack the house. We were defenseless.

Our three meals a day were now rationed to being served twice a day and cooked once a day with no more formal setting. Before the super storm, the servants were not allowed to sit with the masters. In this situation, everyone was equal, and it made me happy. I think Betty figured it out when I would sit with Vilma or JR, the driver, at the servant dining area. I felt sad for them to be eating alone in the midst of a crisis. JR had to sleep inside the car blocking the broken gate. The house had an open garage and the only shield were the cars blocking the entrance. Another iron gate locked the entrance of servants' quarters and kitchen. We were locked out from the main house.

The following night I was getting anxious, so the servant and I decided to sleep on the kitchen floor with the Iron Gate next to the garage. It was so dark, not even starlight. I had another phobia attack. I got up and hid under a small table until daylight. I could not wait to see the early morning light come. I wanted to write, but did not want to use all the candles, we needed that. God help us. Darkness and the known elements lurking outside agitated me. I did not want to hang around in anticipation of nightfall with all the dreadful thoughts of the unknown in the darkness.

Our food supply and cooking gas were getting low. The charcoal would only last another week or less. To help engage my mind, I helped Vilma in the kitchen cooking, and we fried all the meat, fish, and tidied up the house. The continuing rains were a blessing; we collected the rainwater for cooking and drinking, but more rain was also flooding the house. Would we die of starvation, dehydration, or from the diseases in the contaminated waters?

Long hours of darkness. I saw the moon slowly turn as its soft, white light peeked out from the thick clouds. It was a new moon and not very bright, although a relief to the complete darkness as the night passed slowly, despairing.

It was a nice evening, but the fear I could not shake. I ached for my husband and children, wondering if I would be one of those floating, lying dead they would see on TV. My family must be wondering if I would ever see them again. I had been imagining how, during Katrina, the people there did not have any idea if they would ever get help. Now I can relate to them.

Shoot on Site

Today I felt less anxious, and the weather seemed to go along with my spirits, a very nice, sunny day. During breakfast, we discussed our options to abscond. After breakfast, I helped Vilma clear the table, and she started getting our food packed for our journey to Manila as PJ and JR checked the fuel of two cars. We found neither had enough diesel to get very far, almost certainly not even out of town. Diesel on the island was now under rations and perhaps unobtainable, and word was traveling through the neighborhoods that another group of looters and the National People Army (communist rebels) were expected to hit the family's neighborhood at any time.

I felt my heart beat in me like the wheels of a train; the poundings of my heart were bearing me onward toward the unknown. We might believe we were secure, but yet Tacloban was no longer the same. Many dangers and illnesses were afoot to remind us of our destiny. At a final point, we decided that we could not hang about at home much longer. We would have to leave to have a chance at survival. JR ventured into the chaos to try to find some fuel, just before the government issued a shoot-on-sight curfew at starting at 6:00 P.M.

At the same time as I was waiting for everyone to get ready for our two-day journey to Manila, I borrowed a machete from a neighbor and started chopping, hacking, as best I could the fallen mango tree that was blocking the road at the exit of the subdivision. The noon sun was at its peak, and it was well over ninety degrees. I was bathed in sweat from head to foot, and my face was running with perspiration. I continued to feel my strength and willpower oozing out of me. My shoulders, arms, and back ached painfully, and my hand was numb and blistered.

After hours of chopping the mango tree to make a path for our SUV, I had succeeded. This work kept my mind engaged while we were waiting for the right time to leave. Citizens in the neighborhood were not burdened, no matter what, and I think they were astounded or perhaps a family member had died. I was mystified, almost certainly in shock myself.

Hours of Desperation. I feared that my cousin's home would be the object for the looters, so I fled the house, wandered around, and came upon a nearby shanty. Fired by the urgency of the situation I knocked loudly on the front door. No one answered so I opened the door with a vacillating hand. I looked inside and called for the young lad named Jeffry that lived with his grandmother there. Jeffry, the lad that I met the day after Haiyan, was the neighborhood watcher and the word-of-mouth reporter.

I was not preparing for the scene that greeted my eyes. In this small, two-bedroom house, an original home of the V & G Subdivision, lived a family of five, a single parent, including a six-year-old girl, and a grandmother who looked like in she was in her nineties, and they looked terrified, just as I was. The house was lighted from the sunlight, poking through the detached roof and dangling ceiling. Their belongings had been tossed about the house by the evil winds. I thought this would be the last house the looters would turn upside down, so I asked if I could hang about with them.

They were very pleasant and let me pass the time. Moreover, while I waited, I read a book to the six-year-old girl. In anticipation at last, I saw the black SUV belonging to my cousin return home. JR had been scouting the best route to get out of Tacloban. It had been days, my husband and children must be at a standstill. They did not know my whereabouts or if I was living or dead. To these days, all communication systems were down.

My heart sank. My world was beginning to fade out. I said to myself, "I miss you all so much, my darling, Tim, and my children, Brian, Ian, and AJ. You all must be worried sick about me." I had this feeling of emptiness, desperation, weakness, and I was losing my mind. A neighbor woman was weeping and was pale when she found out the shoot to kill curfew started at 6:00 P.M. An additional neighbor came running to my cousin's house to see if we could wait for them to caravan to Manila, but it was already too late.

The six-seat SUV was full of fuel and checked for our travel. We jammed the back seat with food, water, and suitcases. There was very little room to move around. We were all set to leave before 6:00 P.M. I felt so self-centered for wanting to leave, because my cousin, Betty, wanted to stay and take care of her home and belongings, which I do believe was so much more than she anticipated.

The typhoon with towering waves and extreme velocity of winds had taken some of the family treasures that she had collected over her lifetime and these art pieces were now laid into an amorphous magma. We were now in day five, and we had to search outside of Tacloban for the following reasons: No relief was coming. The abominable odor of death was in the air.

JR, Boy, Betty, PJ, Vilma, and I each took a seat as we readied ourselves to depart the neighborhood. JR drove slowly through the little path of the chopped up mango tree, and we were going to try our best to leave the devastated V&G subdivision and head towards the San Jaunico Bridge. We passed by the rough and ready checkpoint, which was preparing for the 6:00 P.M. shoot-to-kill curfew. I never lived in the Philippines when martial law was enacted decades ago, but I got the sensation of misery for the people that were staying behind.

Astounding Flee. We had to drive very slowly because of the branches, wires, poles, and debris scattered about the streets and nearly blocking our exit from the subdivision, but JR was masterful behind the wheel of the SUV as he drove towards Maharlika Highway, which would take us to the bridge, the closest route for Samar Island.

To our disappointment, this part of the drive was only a couple miles, but it was frightful. There was a mass exodus of people going in opposite directions carrying sacks of rice and eggs; crates full of eggs and other stuff as these men carried them on their shoulders. I was in wonder as I looked through the tinted window—the eggs were not broken, when in fact, everything in Tacloban was in disarray.

We were so close to the people and carts that I was certain we would knock some of them over. Mercifully, we did not. Many other people were sitting around, seeming so mystified, and did not recognize what to do.

Several were finding some way to stay alive; I saw a man with six children and his wife construct a temporary dwelling with debris left by Yolanda.

Tim

November 11, 2013: U.S. and Doha Qatar. I awoke and quickly checked Facebook for any news from the family. Sheryl provided me with a cell phone number, and I quickly gave it a call. PJ, Betty's son, answered the phone and gave it to Emy. I finally heard her voice for the first time in four and a half days. Her voice trembled a little as we spoke for less than a minute. They were in a vehicle and leaving Tacloban. They were on the Leyte side of the San Juanico Bridge waiting to cross the bridge. It was around 9:00 P.M. Tacloban time. Our call ended, and I was so happy, but confused as to why were they waiting at the bridge and not moving.

12:21 A.M.   Sheryl's Facebook post
Thank you, Lord, finally good news from my family. Though the sturdy house was wreck by the super typhoon, it is a relief that they are fine.
I will hold on to this for now. In addition, cherish...For there is hope...
Can't wait to hear their voices...

2:51 A.M.   Messenger: Tim, Sheryl, Sandy, and Kristina
Sheryl: Uncle Tim, please call this number (PJ cell phone).
Tim: Sheryl, thank you for the number. I talked with her and I still have tears of joy in my eyes.
Sheryl: That is great, Uncle Tim. I know the feeling.
Tim: Thanks again for helping us through this
Sheryl: Do not mention it, Uncle Tim. We are family.
Tim: Love you people.

4:35 A.M.   Messenger: Tim, Brian, Ian, AJ, Sandy, and Kristina
Kristina: I was able to talk to PJ...and talk to Tita Emy.

She's ok and she will be going on a land trip to Manila,
Philippines and stay there...she wants to say hi to you
all...and she wants to tell you that she's fine...thank God
all is good...

AJ: thank you

(I had talked to Emy briefly and had notified the boys.
Emy wanted to make sure I told Brian "Happy Birthday"
from her.)

Brian: Thanks, love you, mom. When is she coming back?

Tim: We did not discuss that. Talked for a few moments.
She will call when they get to Manila.

I was able to contact Emy via PJ's cell phone when I awoke this morning. They were allowed to cross the bridge and were now in Samar as they
headed to Manila. I left for work feeling much better.

6:10 A.M.   Tim's Facebook post
                 I just talked with Emy Cajipe-Matthews. She & her family
                 are ok, considering what they went through.

Emy

It had taken us about ten hours to reach San Juanico Bridge. We were stuck
in a massive traffic jam and the sun was setting and the skies were darken-
ing. It was a stop and very little go, and I was getting perturbed. Only one
lane was passable, but people were attempting to go in both directions.
Daredevils on motorcycles were able to zip through any little pocket as
they tried to escape.

All of a sudden, an intolerant driver of a car followed a motorcycle
that zipped around us. JR had a notion that there was a passageway, so he
pulled out and followed the motorcycle and car, but there was no passage
and we came to a stop. The driver of the car behind us got out of his vehicle
and approached JR's door, and then he slapped our car window. He hit it
with immense strength, and I feared it might blow apart, but it did not.

There was stillness in our SUV; we were terrified and did not know what the man might do. I was fearful and tremulous in the seat next to Vilma. I had no idea what might come about in the darkness of this war zone. My passport, driver's license, cash, and a credit card were in a little pouch that I wore around my neck. I slowly removed it from my neck tucked it away under the seat. JR remained unruffled and did not act in response to the man, and I appreciated JR for not challenging the dire circumstances. It was a very apprehensive split second before the man finally returned to his vehicle.

Tim

4:00 P.M.   Tim: Hi Sheryl, hope you woke up to good news about your in-laws. Have you heard if the family started their journey to Manila?

Sheryl: There is no news yet, Uncle Tim, still looking forward for positive news. I have called Mom, talked to her an hour ago. They are already inside the barge and are on their way to Manila.

Tim: Not sixty seconds ago, I was thinking you about your in-laws and I received your message. Do not give up hope Sheryl. You are in my prayers.

Sheryl: Thank you, Uncle Tim.

Tim:Have you any news of your in-laws?

Sheryl: I have not yet. Seeking help from friends

6:33 P.M.   Tim's message to Emy

So happy you are out of Tacloban and so nice to hear your voice again. Do you have your passport? Please come home, love you.

9:27 P.M.   Tim's message to Emy

Darling how are you now? Sheryl says you have left Samar and are now on a barge. Hope your travels are safe. Love you.

When they got to the northern tip of Samar, they had to take a barge to the next island called Matnog Sorsogon, Bicol in the Luzon province. Emy remembers that the waters were very rough and rocked the barge from side to side.

10:40 P.M.   Tim's Facebook post
I sit here in my chair knowing my wife and family are surviving a terrible nightmare. Some friends I have heard from are safe while others have not been as fortunate. This disaster has brought me closer to my family. Please keep praying for the folks in Tacloban. Another late night as I sit and think about life and the past week. I head to bed and say my prayers.

Emy

Moment of Trepidation: Vilma, the asthmatic family servant next to me, began to hyperventilate, but I managed to relax her. I had her breathe into the plastic grocery bag that carried our snacks. I simulated deep, slow breaths, in and out, to her, and she was able to follow along and at last began to settle down. I was terrified for a split second that I would be setting next to a corpse all the way to Manila.

It was a difficult drive from the house to the foot of the San Jaunico Bridge. The drive would take twenty minutes on an average day. This was obviously not an ordinary day, and this trip took the better part of ten hours as we traveled through hell and into the darkness. We were all quiet. Usually PJ would be blaring Niki Menaj music, but this drive was solemn.

I still had not seen any local government officials or help from anywhere. Certainly, they must know by now what happed to Tacloban. Why had they not sent help by now? Where are the hundreds of soldiers the president mentioned during his visit the third day after Haiyan? Little did I know how pervasive the damage was from Yolanda.

We spent hours in this traffic jam beneath humid, pouring rains, and I was still wondering if it had been a good option to leave the house. Would we make it to the bridge and into Samar? Finally, the rains were letting up, and we saw three or four military men attempting to direct traffic on this muddled road.

At San Juanico Bridge, more looters had taken to the ships wrecked during the storm. Floating bodies glimmered in the moonlight and the waves gently moved the bodies ashore. Through the reflection of the moonlight and the shimmering light of water, I glanced down at the bay and saw a lifeless woman holding her deceased child floating in that moonlit bay as the gentle waves rocked their body ashore. I felt a cold water pour over me, my head felt so tight. It wasn't fear, but I sensed my mind emptying.

Concerned Family Messages

Messenger: Tim, Brian, Ian, AJ, Garret, Sheryl, Sandy, and Kristina
Garret:They are in Legaspi City, Bicol right now taking a rest at the meantime.
Sandy: Thanks you, brother, for the update,
Sheryl: Hi brother, BB, arriving in Manila 9:00 A.M. tomorrow at Clark Airport
Garret: Sandy/she, advised the family of William and San Kan Marvin to get out of Tacloban at the meantime. Advise them to go to Cebu or Catbalogan and or Calbayog. Samar is chaos and Tacloban is full of uncertainty. Thats the best advice I could give right now.
Sheryl: That is the plan. Thank you
Sandy: Yes Brother, I am still trying to reach Marvin. I already advised his brother also, if they will be contacted by them, to advise evacuation immediately. Thanks!
Garret: Cebu or Manila would be the best choice.
Sandy: Yes, brother, thank you.

6:40 P.M.   Messenger: Tim and Sheryl
Tim: Have they been located yet? (Referring to her in-laws)

Sheryl: Yes, they are already been located, Uncle Tim. We are relieved. We are on our way to the airport. Travel time 9 hours from Qatar to Manila, Last update of Tita Emy, they will be staying in Legaspi for a while.

Tim: So happy for your good news, I hope they are safe. Safe travels for you.

1:42 P.M.   Sheryl's Facebook post
Praise to you, Oh Lord. Thank you for an answered prayer for saving the family. We finally heard news from mother after four days of long silence.

7:40 P.M.   Tim's message to Emy
Darling you are about six hrs from Manila. I respect you for wanting to go to the U.S. Embassy. I really hope you can get some sleep. Please come home. We all miss you.

Emy

Self-determination. The getaway to Manila took us two days, including an overnight stay, but it is approximately 360 miles by air. The San Jaunico Bridge is 2.16 kilometers (1.34 miles) long and connects the Island of Leyte and Samar across the San Jaunico Strait. It is the longest bridge in the Philippines, built during the Marcos era in the mid 1960s, and it provides an important form of transportation between the two islands.

Surprisingly, Typhoon Yolanda did not significantly damage the bridge, and it provided me with the escape route I needed to get out of Tacloban after the storm. Since the storm, the bridge is still one of the most critical gateways for transportation of relief goods and for the evacuating refugees.

We left at four in the afternoon and reached the foot of San Jaunico Bridge at three in the morning the next day. At the foot of San Juanico Bridge on the Leyte side, I noticed cars, trucks, pedestrians were not crossing the Bridge. The traffic jam was just going around Tacloban. As we headed towards Santa Rita, Samar, it was quiet with no traffic. We were the only car driving out of Tacloban; the Samar coast was still sleepy, although in the town of Santa Rita the devastation was substantial. However, when we entered Western Samar coast, it was serene. Only bananas were uprooted and a few house were with no roof. They were spared the worst of the major destruction.

At the crack of dawn, we saw lights the town of Tarangnan, Samar. We stopped at a gas station that was dark and saw people with plastic containers trying to get some gas, but they were out of diesel. In a dimly lit corner, I saw a steam coming from the people gathered around a little stand. A woman was baking bread, pandesal, in an open stove made of clay and fired by wood, the finest pandesal that I ever had. For a moment, it made me accept wisdom about the horror behind us. After a short break, we continued on our journey for Manila.

It concerned me that after the bumper-to-bumper drive along Maharlika highway to San Juanico Bridge, we were the only car barreling out the Maharlika, Samar highway. It felt eerie as we climbed the zigzagged roads leading to the mountains and down to the Catbalogan City seaport. It was still daybreak in the capital of Samar Province, Philippines. Catbalogan City, often referred to as the "gateway to the Samar Region," was spared by the storm surge.

The mountain landscape overlooking the bay in the horizon was awe-inspiring as we drove in. After Haiyan, Catbalogan is now the center of commerce and the financial hub for Tacloban survivors, as it is about a two and a half hours drive from Tacloban. We stopped for more gas; they too were rationing the diesel.

Tim and My Concerned Family in the U.S.

12:07 P.M.   Messenger: Tim, Brian, Ian, and AJ
                Tim: Do u know if Mom made it to Manila?
                Ian: I want to say yes.
                AJ: Haven't heard.
                Tim: I think she is at the Manila Hotel. I have not made contact yet.

A cousin of mine had passed away last week, and my mother and sister would be arriving at my home after lunch so the three of could attend the viewing in Sturgis, which is a short, thirty minutes away. When I arrived home, they were sitting on my back step, and I immediately started to cry as I tried to tell them about Emy's journey. I finally settled down a bit, and we were able to eat a little snack and talk. I was checking Facebook Messenger frequently looking for new developments.

2:11 P.M.	Messenger: Tim and Sheryl
	Tim (10:37 P.M.) Happy you made it to Manila. Still work to be done. I pray your husband finds his family and returns to Manila safely. Have your parents arrived yet? How and where are Sandy and Tintin?
Sheryl:	Yes, they are here already. Did not stay at the hotel with Tita Emy coz Dad wanted to see his grandchildren, especially that we will be going back after we finally settled the whole family here. Uncle Tim, parents told me Tita Emy is very traumatized especially that they saw a woman who died in the middle if labor...the baby's head was about to come out. Boththe mother and baby died in the middle of labor.
	Tim: I am so sad, thanks for the news. Would you know hotel where she is in?
	Sheryl: She is in Manila Hotel, Uncle Tim.
	Tim: Thanks Sheryl, I did talk with her
3:21 P.M.	Messenger: Tim, Brian, Ian, AJ, Garret, Sheryl, Sandy, and Kristina
	Brian: Hello cousins, do any of you know by chance if my mom went to a hotel or anything? I am going to try to contact her.
	Sheryl: Hi Brian, she is in Manila Hotel. When you people see her, please give her a lot or attention and TLC. She has been traumatized the most, my parents said.
	Brian: Okay, I did talk to her, and I understand for sure. Thank you, Sheryl.

AJ: (sad face icon)

3:44 P.M.   Messenger: Tim, Brian, Ian, and AJ
                   Tim: I think she is at the Manila Hotel. + 011(63) 632 527
                   0011 Have not made contact yet.

Emy

Picturesque peak and seaboard. We disembarked toward the next town along Maharlika highway to the mountainside of San Jorge; the town was famous for its Blanca, Aurora falls, near Barangay aurora and Aurora River. The morning sun was now rising, its orange glow on the horizon. It was about 6:00 A.M. The gasoline station was closed.

We were lucky to be the first to arrive when the station opened a little after six. The gas was by now rationed; there was a long line behind us while we were waiting for it to open. We had a chance to stretch our legs and get some crackers and water from a nearby corner store. The store was dark; the window was screened in chicken wires with a little square opening, enough for goods and money handling.

Most of the little store was made that way as I observed. The gasoline boy filled the SUV gas tank about three thousand pesos, equal to seventy-five dollars. In the remoteness of *San Jorge,* the countryside was covered with coconuts and bananas. We were bearing north of Samar. At daybreak, the golden sunlight was rising in the horizon, the sea was calm and as the countryside landscape was a field of blue, green, and violet colors. It was a pleasant, sun-drenched day.

We were the only car barreling down the road from the mountains going down towards the coastline the City of Calbayog. The coastline was so stunning with never-ending sandy beaches. It lay along the coastal region of the province, stretching about 60 miles (97km) from the northern tip of the island and 180 miles (290km) from southern boundary. Calbayog was the most populated city on the island, and was the heart of business and exchange for the entire island. Its airport and seaport made it a supreme place of opportunity for Samar.

At the end of the endless shorelines lay the shores of Allen, Northern Samar, and safe passageway to the main island city of Manila. Suddenly it was a grimy, overcast day; the sun was now hiding in and out of the gray clouds. Allen municipality was situated in the northwestern tip of the province of northern Samar, the northern province of the three provinces compromising Samar Island.

Allen was known for being an imperative port for inter-island transport, distinctively the island of Samar and the big island Luzon. It has been purposeful to transport relief goods from Manila to the devastated Guiaun, Samar and Tacloban, Leyte.

We stopped for lunch at a dimly lit snack bar and had sandwiches while waiting for the ferry to depart. The rain was now pouring hard, big drops of rain. The blustery weather was picking up, and the ocean was getting jerky. It was the fifth day after the tempest; the ferry was not that full, about three cars and two passenger buses. I felt myself unwind since it was not swarming. In my accepted wisdom, we are lucky to get out of Tacloban, but it felt so heartrending for the others that did not have the wherewithal to get out the devastation of Samar and Leyte but to be on familiar terms with their destiny.

Commuter boat traversing; soon we were on board; JR drove onto the car ferry to cross to Matnog. We could not even see beyond the prow of the boat. The air was gray, the ocean looked gray—a very sad, mourning gray. JR parked the car, and we disembarked and ascended the stairwell upstairs. It was stormy as I walked around to situate myself. The ferry peripatetic transversed and rocked perpendicularly like the ferry was in a tug of war, dodging the waves. We were cruising in at about fifty knots, crossing the San Bernardino Strait.

I thought I would be secure if I sat next to a safety boat. The way I looked at the ferry, it was going perpendicularly with the waves and seemed the only means as we traversed for an hour and a half the San Bernardino Strait. I glanced down at the sea and saw it bubbling like a steaming cauldron. It was rough.

Another anxiety set in so I thought I had better sit next to the rubber dingy in case the ferry turned over. It had been a known fact that some ferries capsized crossing the channel. I was now beginning to sound like a survival guru. I was just feeling relaxed and situated as we got closer to Manila when a disconcerting news broadcast came up on the ferry TV. Some New People's Army men had attacked a military detachment in the province of Sorsogon.

Oh my God, I prayed quietly, please do not let it be. The port of Matnog is in Sorsogon, leading to Manila. We were now heading face to face with more elements. I was shaken, and my heart sank. I was beginning to fade out. I closed my eyes and prayed to God for our safety. The car ferry reached the Sorsogon port safe and sound.

Emy

Matnog Sorsogon Bicol province: We drove out to a paved road past rice paddies being worked on by water buffalo that looked like they'd been working for centuries. Once in awhile, I saw some machinery, which I felt happy about. Some more sign of life disparity, a towering house next to a nipa hut or dilapidated house. This was my first land trip from Tacloban, Leyte to this part of the Bicol region Luzon province, sitting in the backseat, jam-packed with our belongings. I thought it would be nice to stay and spend a day sightseeing and get closer to Mayon Volcano. It was so beautiful from afar.

The rain finally stopped as we reached the Legaspi City at the foothills of Mayon Volcano. It was so majestic. It was now 6:00 P.M., and we stopped for dinner at a mall off the highway. The city was bustling. It looked clean and organized. We walked around the mall looking for a liquor store. I had been craving Merlot or any red wine I could find. I am a social drinker, but I sounded alcoholic at this time. For my delight, I did not have to go very far; as I enter the glass double door there, it was on my left. I found the wine I was looking for and bought two bottles, a spare in case of emergency.

I am again a happy camper. My energy is back and we started looking for a hotel to stay at. We did not need a map from Tacloban to Allen Northern Samar. However, as we crossed to Sorsogon, they had few veins of roads, so JR would stop anyone along the way to ask for directions. Thank God, after driving around in this new city, we found the gated Alicia Hotel just off the highway from the city of Legaspi. Comfortable and accommo-dating, the hotel compound was big in three separate buildings.

The family section was across the street where Boy, PJ, and JR had a room and no bathtub. Betty, Vilma, and I got a room with bathtub. Our hotel was across the street from the main building; our room was on the second floor from the lobby to the right of a conference room. To the left was a wide stairwell to the second floor rooms. The hotel was quiet, dim, and seemed empty.

It was welcoming to see happy faces, the faces that I did not see in the past five days in Tacloban. The hotel was beautiful. I could see it through the glass wall and glass door as we approached the counter. The hotel clerk, a helpful young woman, read us all the amenities. They had a selection of group rates for the hotel stay, day excursions to the beautiful Legaspi City, and a buffet. It was so comforting to hear breakfast announcement and my appetite was back. I could not wait until morning.

I was feeling relieved and temporarily forgot the elements that we been through. My back was sore from sitting cramp in the SUV, and my swollen knee nagged. I absolutely had a feeling of exhilaration. I asked for a massage service in our room that we needed very much to get the tension out and be glad we were all fine. Pure bliss came into my mind, thank you Lord.

We checked into two separate rooms and planned to meet in the morn-ing for a nice buffet breakfast and go sightseeing to the Majestic Mayon Volcano. The bellman carried our suitcases to our room and I was excited to settle in, have a hot bath, a soft bed and a good night sleep in the air con-ditioned hotel room. Once I was in our hotel room I was ready to jump into a long, hot bath, armed with a bottle of Merlot and a wine glass.

My excitement was suddenly interrupted when I saw a disconcerting news bulletin on TV. The caravan of relief food available for the typhoon survivors had been surprise attacked by gunmen who took the relief food with them, creating even more of a dilemma for delivering the goods; I did not think I could be in this world through this. I had a bottle of wine and it gave me a temporary numbing of my edginess. My lower back seized up more in these few days. It has been awhile since I had indulged my desires for a massage.

Betty, Vilma and I had massages in our room. For two days we sat with our nerves tightening. We needed some relaxation; for a while my worries disappeared. I got a call from my husband, Tim, followed by my son, Ian. It was a relief to hear my family's voices of comfort. I just listened in without interlude as tears rolled down my face. My heart ached as I certainly soaked up the sensation. I never talked about anything from my experiences, for it just made me sadder.

It has been two months since I had had a hot bath, and it was wonderful. I must have soaked in the hot bath three times the whole night. Still I was having nightmares. This time was getting much worse listening to the latest news. My whole being was again in turmoil.

Nightmarish November 12, 2013: Legaspi City Bicol, in the early morning at around 2:00 A.M., a nightmare attack. The hotel was moving. I woke up sweating, my heart pumping hard. I was scared and petrified and decided to soak in a warm bath. I got dressed and look out the window. It was dark; I saw in the dark shadows someone sitting below a garden umbrella. He must be the security guard. I walked downstairs to the front desk. It was dark, and no one was around. I went back to the hotel room and called the front desk. No answer, which made me so fretful that I woke up everybody and prepared to go.

I walked across the street in the dark; I saw a guard sleeping in the shed. I found Boy having an elevated temperature. Betty was in attendance of him. I woke the security guard and asked him to get someone to check out early. We waited until Boy was feeling recovered to finish the last leg of our journey to Manila. We started at first light in that depressing misty morning, and rain started pouring hard. The hotel boy filled our thermos with coffee and pandesal from the day before for breakfast. We stopped for gas and off we went.

It was almost noon. JR missed a turn off and took a scenic zigzag road instead of the short cut. We lost few miles of travel and torrential rain started pouring hard. We decided to wait and have lunch in Lucena. After lunch and a good rest, the sun peeked from behind the silvery clouds. The rain stopped as we traveled to Manila. For two days we hardly talked. It was so tense, probably because we were all in a state of shock. My fear was taking control of me and the whole situation. Betty was somewhat bewildered with my actions.

In the two days that it took to reach Manila, Philippines on the main island of the country, I felt like I surpassed the four elements of terror, but made it to Manila and I would eventually fly home. Tears stained my cheeks, reminding me keenly of how alive I was just now.

5:32 A.M.   Messenger: Tim and Emy

Emy:Thanks so much for all your concern. I am doing fine but the nightmare will linger. I am sad for all my dearest Philippine family, friends, and all the people in Leyte and Samar and the Visayan region toppled by Haiyan. More horrifying stories to tell, some of them will always linger in my mind as long as I live. Thank you all and thank you God for keeping me, my family and to all those unfortunate people who were not able to escape this tragedy, May God Bless us all.

Tim: Darling you are connected? I tried calling but no answer. Did Betty come and help? Do you have your plane ticket? Love you.

Emy:My iPad is not working, cannot Skype. Love you. Yes, Betty is here with me.

Tim: Do you have your plane ticket?

Emy: I have a ticket but trying to find the copy

7:32 A.M.   Messenger:Tim, Brian, Ian, and AJ

Tim:Just talked with Mom. Betty is with her again and is feeling a little more relaxed. She is working on a plane ticket. Love you.

Ian: Ok good! Thx dad.

Tim:Hotel # = 011 632 527 0011

Tim

Before leaving for my cousin's viewing, I was able to talk to Emy at the Manila Hotel. It was so nice to finally talk to her for more than a couple of minutes. We had much to talk about, but she had another problem now.

Her credit card had expired; she had very little cash left, and she did not know what to do. I had her new credit card at home, but that was not helping. I called the credit card company, explained the situation, and asked them if they could change the expiration date. They could not, but offered to send new cards to her in 7–10 business days. That would not help either.

I called the hotel again and gave them my name and the reason why I was calling. "Yes, Mr. Tim. How may we help you?" I explained that I had Emy's credit card here and asked what I need to do for them to accept the credit card. They said I could email them a copy of the front and back and that would be okay. "Thank you so much!"

I called Emy again to update her on this development, and I told her I would call her after the viewing.

After we arrived at the church, I checked my phone for messages. I had an email from the Manila Hotel indicating they had received my email and everything was okay now. That put my mind to ease as we walked into the viewing area and saw all the people morning the loss of my cousin. Several of my relatives came to me to ask about Emy, and again I cried. It was nice to see all the nice people again.

1:03 P.M.   Tim's message to Emy
               Good morning Darling, I Love You. All of Whitewood
               folks say hi to you & get home soon.

1:54 P.M.   Messenger: Tim & Carmyn Egge
               Carmyn:
               http://www.state.gov/p/eap/ci/rp/typhoon/index.htm#
               Here's some helpful information for you. Thinking of
               you!!
               Tim: Thanks Carmyn
               Carmyn: Also this one -
               http://google.org/personfinder/2013-yolanda/
               Tim: Yes I actually used this
               Carmyn: Good! I am thinking of you both! Let me know

if I can be helpful! XOXOXO

Tim: Thank you, it was nice to see Nyla & Gen again

Carmyn: Mom said it was good to see you as well. I sent along some hugs for you, I hope she delivered.

Tim: You know she did! Thank you so much. Just had a nice talk with Emy, hoping to get her on a plane ASAP. Love you.

Carmyn: That is wonderful news!

Emy

Manila Hotel Sanctuary: My cousin dropped me off at Manila Hotel by the bay, a block away from the U.S. Embassy. They drove off to nearby Quezon City, where they had a third home. I checked in at Manila Hotel, a Philippine landmark, a stately turn of the century hotel. It has a view of the Manila Bay sunset. Nearby are the fortress of Corregidor, the poignant ruins of the medieval fortress of Intramuros and a promenade to Luneta Park. It has a guard that checked everyone in the car with his sniffing dog behind. I feel reassured.

The hotel was opulent inside. No dimness here, it was lit up like a Christmas tree and bustled with foreigners in designer gym clothes and formal attire. For a moment I thought I was home in the U.S. The door attendant greeted me and put my luggage on a conveyor, like at the airport, for safety precaution. The hotel employees were dressed in Filipino garb, looking like movie stars. Inside the hotel were marble floors, a body-scanning arch gate check that lead the main entrance. I could hear live music blaring from a nearby club. There was a huge waiting area with tables and "reserved" signs from all over the world. It was quite impressive and beautiful and newly renovated and added a new section preserving the old side facing the Manila Bay.

I remember when I was in college, a group of my friends stayed here for a weekend. I felt at home; I breathed a sigh of relief. The concierge took my luggage and the very nice receptionist had a room available in the old wing for six thousand a night. I was bewildered when I heard six thousand until I realized she meant pesos not dollars. That would be about $150. After I checked in, Betty was feeling relieved, along with Boy, JR, and Vilma, who all left to a nearby Quezon City.

My hotel room was in the old part overlooking Manila Bay on the third floor. It was beautiful, with two queen-sized beds for Betty and me. After checking into my hotel room, I went back to the receptionist and I asked for the computer room. I was anxious to connect with my family. Each visit to the computer room I had to pay in cash, for it was a separate entity from the hotel charges. My iPad and phone had been drenched by the super typhoon, so the main communication to my family was ruined.

The reception clerk called another clerk to usher me past the international hall with reserved tables for different countries, up a few steps to the right, she unlocked the glass door to the computer room and gave me a password and took a twenty-five dollar fee each time. I sat at console to connect with my family in the U.S., while she sat in the adjoining room, waiting for me to be done so she can lock up.

I regard as out of tribulations, knowing they have safety measures and sniffing dogs. At Manila Hotel, my family was certainly at ease; Brian, my birthday son, must have called me three times that day, following a call from my husband, Tim, my relatives and friends in the U.S. assured of my safety. I talk to Ian briefly, but the youngest, AJ, had not called me at all. I found out later that he was distraught the whole time I was missing for five days. Nevertheless, I was feeling mentally drained; on and off my brain was drifting away. I was afraid of losing my mind, being away from my family to remind me who I am, a very disturbing thought. I kept my passport, license, a credit card, and cash in a pouch around my neck.

Consternation Attack Night: alone after a chat with my husband, I stopped at the hotel bar for a glass of wine, and went back to my room for a hot bath and hoped I would sleep well. Another nightmare woke me, still I was not able to sleep. I got up, got dressed, went downstairs, and sat in the lobby and read the paper until the breakfast buffet opened. The buffet catered to international guests. They had everything I could think of the day after Haiyan that I felt so hungry. I must have devoured everything I missed. Afterward, I sat at the lobby to wait for Betty. I did not see a recognizable face; I felt in the vein of having lightheadedness.

Tim

My mother, sister, and I had a little coffee and a light breakfast as we discussed my call with Emy last night. In a short time, we would head to Sturgis for the funeral. The service was nice, but my mind was occupied with Emy. I needed to get her home. After the service, we went to Whitewood, South Dakota for a reception, and we talked with our relatives again. Aunt Thelma, the mother of the deceased, was so concerned about Emy while grieving for the loss of her child.

After the reception, my mother, sister, and I drove back to Rapid City, where they packed up their Suburban and headed out on their four-hour drive home. I hopped on the computer to look for new information. I saw an amazing offer from Verizon, offering free calls from the U.S. to the Philippines. I called Verizon to confirm what I saw, and the person was not aware of this policy. He checked, and said yes, this was true. Wow, how nice of them, I thought. I think AT&T offered a similar program.

2:35 P.M. Tim's Facebook post
      Verizon is offering free calls from U.S. to the Philippines
      until Dec 7. AT&T does as well but not sure of the dates.
      Very nice of them.

I immediately called the Manila Hotel and gave them my name. "Yes, Mr. Tim, how may help you?" (I enjoyed the Mr. Tim part.) I asked for Emy's room, and she was there. We talked for over an hour, and it was most comforting. She would work with Delta Airlines to get a flight to the United States. Yes, I was finally thinking she would be home in a few days. The storm surge from Haiyan had taken her phone, so she would not be able to contact us when she arrived.

I called Gladys, Emy's cousin in Oakland and gave her an update about Emy. I let her know Emy was at the Manila Hotel and was planning to arrive in San Francisco tomorrow. Gladys said she would go to the airport and try to find Emy during her three-hour layover. I was so happy that a familiar face would be there to meet Emy.

2:40 P.M.   Sandy's Facebook post
                 The best morning wake-up call ever! I'm so glad to finally
                 hear your voice at the other end of the line. I thank the
                 Lord for keeping you safe and your family. I will see you
                 soon. I Love You Honey!

3:39 P.M.   Messenger: Tim, Brian, Ian, and AJ
                 Tim: Just talked with Mom. Doing much better, had some
                 laughter. Hope to get her on a plane today. Free AT&T and
                 Verizon calls to Philippines. I may come get her in Cali-
                 fornia then fly home to South Dakota. Love you.
                 Brian: That would be awesome if you came out. I can pick
                 you up in Las Vegas if it is cheaper.
                 Tim: I will do some checking.
                 Tim: I will call Mom in a few hours, hoping she has flight
                 info. What hotels are close to you?
                 Brian: On Google, search "lodgings near 92011." There
                 are a bunch of hotels that come up but the LA Quinta and
                 the Ramada I think seem best and are right across the free-
                 way from us. Google says about $60/night.
                 Tim: Cool, thanks for checking.

7:27 P.M.   Messenger: Tim, Sheryl, Sandy, and Kristina
                 Tim: You will always be in my heart. Praying you are okay.
                 Sheryl: (thumbs up icon)

I awoke earlier than normal Friday morning and quickly grabbed my
phone from the nightstand so I could check for a message from Emy. Yes,
there it was, a brief message telling me she got a plane ticket and would be
leaving Manila early the next day and would arrive in San Francisco on
Saturday morning at 8:40 A.M. This was very confusing to me with the fif-
teen-hour time difference, but I would figure that out later.

4:42 A.M.   Emy's message to Tim
                 I got a flight. Delta Sat. 16 Nov. @7:40 A.M. Manila to

Tokyo Delta 162
Tokyo-Narita/San Francisco Delta 208 8:40 A.M.
Leave SF 12:00N arrive 1:25 P.M. Los Angeles Delta 5841
See you all soon. Love you.

5:03 A.M.   Tim's message to Emy
      Love u

Later in the day, I received her flight information from the Manila Hotel. I got out of bed and went to the computer to purchase a plane ticket to Los Angeles so I could meet Emy and comfort her. I found a flight leaving Rapid City on Saturday morning around 10:00 A.M. that would get me into LAX thirty minutes before Emy. How perfect and convenient is that? I decided we would stay in Carlsbad, CA for a few days and return home on Wednesday.

Tim: Mom will be arriving Los Angeles on Sat. 16 @ 1:25 P.M.
Tim: Would it be better to fly in to Los Angeles or Carlsbad for me?
Tim: I will arrive LAX at 1:00 P.M., then find Mom, yeah. We will leave LAX Wednesday morn. need ride.
Brian: Okay.
Tim: Brian will you arrange transportation?
Brian: Okay.
Tim: Reserve a room at Ramada. Mom will go through customs at San Francisco International Airport, I would guess. Gladys will try to meet her.
AJ: When is she in San Diego?
Tim: She arrives LAX, as do I. Can u pick us up there? Should we fly to Carlsbad?
AJ: And what day and time would Mom arriving?
Tim: Sat 1:30 P.M. at LAX
Tim: Flight from LAX to Carlsbad was too much.

6:50 A.M   Tim's message to Emy
      Darling I will be in LAX tomorrow to meet you. So happy.

Emy

The hotel employees where very helpful. They made all the arrangements for my flight and saved me three hundred dollars for flying out of the country sooner that my previous itinerary. They made me feel at ease. I merely sat near the reception and drank some tea. For a moment, I was feeling in distress so I walked to the reception counter for help. As I got closer, a clerk became aware of me falling. He took hold of me and sat me on a chair.

Soon after, I remember waking up at the Manila hotel clinic with nurses around me. I had a minor attack of depression and high blood pressure; I was unable to find my mind. My body at a final point had given up from the horror I left behind in Tacloban. The storm surge, the elements, fear of darkness, the brutal and overwhelming experience I had underwent were physically too much, and yet beyond a certain point, I do not know how to convey its violence except by piling one adjective onto another, so that in the end I should convey no expression at all except perhaps of embarrassing exaggeration. It took me some time to grasp the deep-seated reason for this weakness.

Tim called again to see how I was and was told I had a minor depression and unstable high blood pressure. He found out I was unaccompanied and instantaneously called Betty to come up and be with me. At the Manila Hotel clinic, my cousin, Gladys from Richmond, CA, kept me company on the phone; she helped alleviate a lot of my susceptibility.

Betty was not able to stay with me the first night we arrived at Manila hotel, for she also had some family that flew in, Sheryl, her husband William, and their two young children, from Doha Qatar just to be with them at this time of predicament, which I truly understand with no regrets. We were all vulnerable, as it was a nightmare. Betty stayed with me that night. We had dinner at the hotel restaurant. We had duck liver with cranberry sauce for an appetizer and had wine. Our dinner entrée was prime rib with rice and vegetables. The night was special for the two us as we celebrated my return home.

November 12, 2013: My days were really exhausting from not getting enough sleep, but I wanted to make the best of it since I will be leaving soon. I will miss my confidant, Betty. We checked the huge buffet—it was all over every corner in a huge section of the hotel. I had eggs benedict. The rest were a variety of international and Filipino dishes for breakfast, lunch, and dinner.

After a big breakfast, on our way out for a walk to stroll the nearby Luneta Park, I stopped at the reception counter to find out how soon I would be leaving for the U.S. Good news from the good-looking receptionist assisting me with my flight reservation back to the U.S. She was so clever she was able to convince Delta Airline not to charge an early departure flight fee of three hundred dollars since my outbound ticket was not until February 2014.

Afterward Betty and I walked down the street and visited the Ocean World Aquarium. I bought us tickets at the kiosk, and we went to the aquarium. It was so crowded and noisy, I was afraid the glass would break anytime soon. Betty and I left, and we walked onto the grandstand to watch the sea otter show, past souvenir shops selling sunglasses, bamboo fans, and stuffed animals, and looked for a place to sit at the Arena. I felt very relaxed; it was getting late, so we headed back to Manila Hotel to wait for our driver Lando.

Lando was already waiting to drive us to dinner; we hopped in the SUV and drove to a seaside restaurant along Roxas Boulevard. We approached a huge, almost empty parking lot behind a wooden blockage. We stopped in a dark stall where a ruddy-looking man came out with a parking pay stub. The seaside restaurant stood on stilts in the water and was long and rectangular in shape, stretching from the seawall out to the open sea of Manila Bay.

The aisle in the middle separated the sitting area into two, at least six tables in one and four in the other; it was all open in the dining area. The ambiance was the Bay and Manila metropolis. The menu had a selection to choose from the Philippines and international cuisines. I had green vegetables cooked in coconut milk, steamed rice, and fried fish sauté in black bean sauce.

Tim

I arrived at work Friday morning and immediately went to my boss's office and tried to tell him I would be gone for a few days. I was so excited about the wonderful news, and I was surprised when I became so emotional that I had to step away from his doorway as I tried to compose myself. After a couple aborted attempts, I finally managed to say, "I have to go get Emy. She is fine; I will be gone for a few days." Jeff did not know how to react to my emotional outburst and said, "Do whatever you need to."

12:00 P.M.   Tim's message to Emy
                Darling I guess you will go through customs in SF not
                LAX. Should we meet at baggage claim?

I did not know if she was on a plane yet or not. I did not know if she would get this.

Emy

Broadcasting tête-à-tête: while in Manila, I heard the news broadcast that the reliefs are not happening for Samar, Leyte, and they wanted to be of assistance on the paramount need to launch the relief. I called the number on the TV screen and had a discussion with Lyn Penzon, a Research Coordinator for DzMM, ABS-CBN. Lyn took some information from me, and I told her my passage out of the confounded Tacloban.

After awhile, Korina/Jasmine Romero of dzMM teleRadio, called for an interview. I wanted to give a complete picture to the media to let them be on familiar terms with the most excellent itinerary to transport commodities to Guiaun, Samar, Tacloban, Leyte, and some other municipalities that been devastated by the strongest tempest in history.

I immediately started crying, remembering all manner of poor souls with misshapen lives I saw while walking in Tacloban before the storm, the beggars and the homeless living in a cardboard boxes. That seemed to have been over and done. Furthermore, we had a discussion about the well-being of the survivors, their psychological distress, as I was having, they would need some mental health doctors, a trauma team, in addition to relief goods.

Manila Hotel, November 13, 2013: I can hardly believe it. I stopped at the desk and ordered a wakeup call for four the next morning. My flight would leave at eight; I wanted to make sure I had plenty of time to check out and check in at the airport. As I left the reception desk, the clerk ordered a bag of complimentary breakfast for me since the patisserie was not open for breakfast that early. At dawn, I told myself I was anxious to leave, but deep in my heart, I was having another nightmare as though the building were moving. I sleep walked out of bed and into the elevator to the reception to check out.

The bellman got my luggage and took it to the waiting service car, which would drop me off to the NAIA. To my dismay, I forgot the departure fee; I bought a one-way ticket for JR, the driver, for Tacloban so he would be with his young family. I gave him my entire stack of pesos to purchase foodstuff and medication to bring back to Tacloban. My card was not accepted, almost certainly waiting for my hotel charges to clear. Thanks to Delta Airlines—they had funds for that circumstance.

As well as, thanks to the woman at the Delta counter for her kindheartedness. I was able to embark the plane on my way home to U.S. I did not have a desire to stay any longer at this time. I contained myself to leave and recuperate. Under any circumstances, in my heart I would be deathly ill if I stayed to lend a hand for the relief effort. I was not being overemotional. It is hard to put into words the horror until after the reality sinks in.

My family had been concerned regarding my well-being the days after the storm with no account of me. My husband, Tim, was calling the Red Cross, the U.S. Embassy, but to no avail. My children were so frenzied posting in the social media concerning their mother who was caught in the eye of Super Typhoon Haiyan. AJ, my youngest who was anesthetized about me, was in seclusion so he did not have to answer questions regarding my whereabouts.

Jim

I awoke Saturday morning around 6:00 A.M., read the paper, and had breakfast. I packed up the Explorer, headed for the airport, and parked in the
long-term parking lot. It was a nice November morning for Rapid City,
but it was to be cold and snowy on our return the following Wednesday, so
I brought along a warm coat for Emy and left it in the Explorer. I packed
light enough so I would not have to check any luggage.

I had actually checked in the night before and had the e-tickets on my
phone, which I had purchased just last month. The phone was most useful
the previous week and simplified many things. I arrived an hour early for
my 10:00 A.M. flight, and I walked around the small airport several times
as I waited for the boarding call. The call finally came, and we boarded the
small plane for the short ride to Denver. We departed on time and I was
pleased. This would work out just fine.

I had a short layover of only thirty minutes in Denver, so after we
landed, I quickly checked the Departure screens to find my next gate. It
was in the same concourse, but at the opposite end of the concourse, though
it would be no problem getting there with time to spare. I was meeting my
wife, so it was all good. I went to the bathroom and headed for the departure
gate. As I approached the seating area for the gate, I saw on the display behind the counter that the flight was now delayed, but it did not say for how
long. My heart sunk as I figured I would now arrive after Emy in Los Angeles International Airport, and she would be alone again.

Gladys had called to let me know she was at the San Francisco Airport
and after several intercom announcements, she had finally found Emy.
What a relief. For the past two days when I had thought about our reunion,
I would get all choked up, teary eyed, and the time for our encounter was
getting closer. What would happen, would we cry? Who knows?

I took a few deep breaths and repeated some words from Joyce Meyers:
"Don't worry about things you have no control over." I then called Brian
to let him know my flight was delayed and asked him to please be at LAX
before 1:30 P.M. and find his mother. I said I would call him as soon as I
knew my departure time. Since there was nothing I could do, I walked

around and got a bottle of water. For about the third time, I checked for the departure time, and it was showing a departure in about thirty minutes. Yeah! I now figured that Emy would arrive fifteen minutes before me.

The flight from Denver to Los Angeles was a nice flight, and I think we gained a little time as we arrived a few minutes early, "Good job, Mr. Pilot!" I grabbed my bag from the storage compartment above my seat and left the plane as quickly as possible. I saw a sign pointing to Baggage Claim and headed that way. Then I saw a security guard and a barricade appearing to be blocking my path to baggage claim. I slowed down and asked the guard how to get to the baggage claim area. He pointed to the other side of the barricade. I am thinking, "all right," no detour yet.

I stepped on to the down escalator as I reached for my phone to call Brian. He answered his phone and says he is at the airport and headed towards the baggage claim. He had not seen Emy yet. I told him I will see him soon and hung up the phone. As I stepped off the escalator and turned left toward the baggage carousels, I see Brian about forty feet away. I continued toward him in a hurried fashion, and our eyes finally met. Once we are close enough, we hug for several moments, and my tears are ready to flow again, but I hold them back. God, it is good to see Brian again.

We stood by one of the baggage carousels and talked while we waited for Emy. Brian and I were talking while turning our heads in every direction looking for Emy. The area was not very busy, so we would be able to see her if she came our way. I turned to look over my right shoulder behind me down a dimly lit hallway. To my surprise, I saw Emy entering the baggage claim area in her famed pink Bebe outfit and a pink hat.

Time now slowed to a crawl as I told Brian, "There she is," and I released the handle of my bag from my left hand. I could see the bag falling in slow motion to the ground. I turned to my right and took a step toward Emy as Brian grabbed my falling bag. She was less than twenty feet away now and nothing was in between us. I looked at her and our eyes met for the first time in months, but I was not sure she saw me.

How could she not see me? We took another step toward each other, and I could tell she finally saw me. My emotions surfaced again when we were just a couple of feet apart and tears started to flow before I even got to her. I finally reached her, and we hugged for what seemed like ten minutes. Finally, we gained our breath and tried to contain our cries of happiness as I saw strangers from the corner of my eye watching us. We finally were able to compose ourselves a little bit, and Emy and Brian enjoyed a wonderful hug.

In fewer than ten minutes of arriving at LAX, the three of us found each other. Thank you, Lord. We collected Emy's luggage and set out in the Los Angeles air to find Brian's car. It was a short walk to the car, and we were talking nonstop. Brian loaded the bags in his newly washed, dark blue Acura as Emy crawled into the back seat. I got in the front passenger's seat while Brian got behind the wheel. We exited the parking garage, entered the 405 on ramp, and headed south to Carlsbad.

Emy

I am so heartbroken over the agonizing situation I have put my family through, wherein my cherished cousin Gladys met me for an epigrammatic break in my journey while I waited for a flight to Los Angeles, where my husband, Tim, flew from Rapid City. I saw my husband as I passed through the customs cordon. My tears finally exploded from my tear ducts, the panic and terror that had been deep inside me for days. So much happiness in my heart, it spilled out my eyes. Tim grabbed me, hugged me, and held me close to him and whispered softly, "I love you so much." I put my arms around his round belly.

I was torn with emotions. I could hardly speak, "I never want to be alone." He was unwearyingly waiting for my homecoming. As for me, I was still sensing the astonishing elements that I outshined, but bearing in mind Tim and Brian's proverbial faces were beautiful and consoling. Our poignant reunion, we were all shuddering and in tears. My eldest son, Brian, drove to LA to meet my husband and me, a soothing sensation.

After an hour or so, we were in Carlsbad, California where all three of my children live. A touching get-together, I on no account wanted to be single-handed ever again; I reunited with my husband and the gents, who were fearfully waiting for my adventure to end. Understanding of ghastliness of my recollection of the revolting elements that I lived through, I have no sentiments but put into words how blessed I am to be living and walking on earth, to be in this world through the wrath of Haiyan, the most wicked typhoon in history. After the storm when all broke loose, in the midst of chaos, I found myself clutching my passport, my lone possession.

November 16, 2013: Because of not having a communiqué for days after Haiyan, my husband and children were unable to help and apprehensive. I felt so ghastly those few days. It was like perpetuity. It is gratifying at this moment that in a time of angst for a disaster like this, family, friends, and people you are not even on familiar terms with will come together to contribute to a universal need. During this catastrophic situation, we made everyone realize that we are in this world together, every soul in this world. At this time of grief, we are all connected.

Tim

My left arm reached to the back seat to touch Emy and hold her hand. She dozed off a couple times during the hour-and-a-half drive to Carlsbad. Brian and I conversed, and he told me of his plans to go back to school and find a new job. Brian had a couple hours before he had to go to work, and he was hungry so we stopped at the Bistro West restaurant in Carlsbad and ate a mid-afternoon dinner.

After we finished eating, Brian took us to their home so he could get ready for work. Brian, Ian, and AJ shared a home together, and it is a cozy situation. We transferred our bags to Ian's car, and he gave Emy a long hug. AJ had previous plans to go camping, so he would not arrive until Sunday afternoon.

3:04 P.M.   Tim's Facebook post
                 Reunited again!

Emy's iPad was damaged from the storm surge in Tacloban, and she tried to turn it on while still in Tacloban, but it would not turn on. Ian's girlfriend, Roylene, put some rice in a dish along with the iPad to see if we could save it, but this did not help. We sat around talking and snacking until about 8:00 P.M. when I saw that Emy was falling asleep on the couch, so I asked Ian to take us to the Ramada Inn. He was not sure where it was, but I told him I know where to go. Unfortunately, I misunderstood the map and did not know where it was. Ian got on his phone and got the directions. He dropped us off at the front office, and he returned home. Emy and I checked in and walked to our room.

Emy was tired, but she wanted to show me a few things she was able to bring with her: some chocolate, a hot chocolate pot, candies, and a newspaper from the Manila Hotel. We lay on the bed and held each other while she told me some of her stories. I could do nothing more than listen and hold her. I showed her my new phone and let her know we could call the Philippines free for a few days. She was tired and fell asleep. I watched a little TV and finally fell asleep as well.

November 17, 2013: In the middle of the night, I woke up to see the light on; Emy was awake and could not sleep. She was talking to a relative in the Philippines. After she hung up, we talked a little more before we dozed off again.

A few hours later, I woke up, took a shower, and went to get some coffee for Emy and me. After we had our coffee, we went for a walk and found a Verizon store in a strip mall. We walked in and there was one associate and one customer, so we took a seat and waited for someone to help us. Emy's phone had been lost in the typhoon, and she needed a new phone. She selected a black iPhone 5 with a white and pink case. All right, she was connected to the world again. We walked across the parking lot to a Panda Express and had something to eat. We called Ian, and he came to pick us up.

We went to the Apple Store to see if they could repair the iPad. They said we would need an appointment and the next one was in three hours. We signed up for the appointment and left the store. As we approach Ian's car, I noticed the tires were almost bald and needed to be replaced now, that he should not wait much longer. He called Sears and made an appointment for new tires. We dropped the car off and waited for Roylene to pick us up, because it would take a few hours to get the work completed.

When we arrived at the boys' home, AJ greeted us. He was home from the camping trip and had just gotten out of the shower, more hugs and conversation. A while later, AJ's girlfriend, Stephanie, came over with some wine. Someone called Emy's niece Athena to come over to see us. AJ took Ian to Sears to pick up his car. Brian had returned from work, so we were all together for the first time.

We missed the appointment at the Apple store and made another for the next day. They would not even attempt to repair it, but they did offer a hundred dollars off a new one. We decided that would be the best option and bought a new one. Many of her pictures from when she was in the Philippines were recovered from the iCloud.

November 18, 2013:

6:40 P.M.   Emy's Facebook post

After five days of sleepless nights and fear in Tacloban, I finally feel safe to be with my husband, who flew in to LA to meet me and be with my loving children.

We hung out at home and we were happy being together. Emy would fall asleep on the couch and check out Facebook on her iPad. The next couple of days ran together, and I cannot remember what we did when.

Tuesday evening, Brian drove us back to the Comfort Inn near LAX. The traffic was bad, and it took over two hours to get there. We checked in and lay on the bed checking for Facebook messages before we fell asleep.

We awoke Wednesday morning, had breakfast, packed, and took the shuttle to LAX. We checked our bags, went through security, and found our terminal. I just wanted to get home. The flight to Denver was fine, and we had a short layover before the final leg to Rapid City.

Emy

As a collective group, these fine young men found a way to work together and raise funds for the victims of Haiyan. Brian, Ian, and AJ of Backlines Training Center, the home of MMA fighters, their UFC champion friends,

Mr. Brandon Vera, Mr. Joey Beltran, sponsored by San Diego Rock FM 105.3. The nobility of these men is so powerful that is so gratifying indeed. In addition, thanks to Verizon for the free calls made to the Philippines in this time of crisis. your generosity is deeply appreciated. To this writing, the disaster relief raised has not arrived. I look forward to that by the time my book is make known, the relief commodities will be in the hands of the deserving people.

While we were in Carlsbad getting ready for our flight home to Rapid City, one of my friends called to see if I would be willing to do an interview with our local newspaper, the *Rapid City Journal*. The local Filipino community wanted to have a benefit dinner to help some of the typhoon survivors and thought it would help if I told my story. I agreed to the interview, and my story was in the paper a couple days before the benefit dinner. The event was very heartwarming and successful. KEVN, a local TV station, covered the dinner and interviewed me as well as some others. Thank you so much, Rapid City.

Jim

Emy and I were home in Rapid City, South Dakota, by 10:00 P.M., and winter was in full force. Cold, blowing snow greeted us. I ran to the long-term parking lot and got in my 1994 Ford Explorer. I paid the attendant and circled around to pick up Emy and the bags. I gave her the winter coat I brought for her, loaded the bags, and headed home.

It would be weeks before she slept all night long. She had problems with nightmares and would wake up almost every night at 2:00 A.M. She spent most of her days reading about the typhoon and the aid that many countries sent, but that did not seem to be reaching the hard hit areas of Leyte. It was painful for me to watch her struggle with all the news. She was expecting Tacloban to be rebuilt in a week, and now months later, it has not returned to the way it was before the typhoon. I told her New Orleans has not yet been restored to pre-Katrina times, and it has been years for them.

Time seems to be helping her, but she still has the occasional sleepless night.

Emy

Conviction and Destiny: I am grateful to God for being alive, for being with my family again, and hoping to revisit to Tacloban and Hinangutdan, Santa Rita, Samar to finish my Resource Center building project, my unfinished scholarship program for the impecunious children. Most importantly, maybe my going back and seeing the improvements of devastation will help ease my restlessness and nightmares. For some mystifying reason, I lost all the video remembrance I took on my iPad. The rest was all there. Could the beloved Lord not want me to have a memory of the Haiyan wrath?

Betty's front door entrance

Chandelier at Betty's house

Betty's main sitting room

Betty's formal dining room

Betty's outdoor pool

Downtown Tacloban

Tacloban

San Jaunico Bridge

Family on San Juanico Bridge 2006

Arriving at Hinangutdon

Hinangutdan street

The Church Simplicio Cajipe built

Inside the church

A house on Hinangutdan

Another house on Hinangutdan

Santa Rita Cemetery

Hinangutdan Elementary School Drum and Marching Band

Roasting a pig on Dabong Island

Fishing Village

Ian collecting a coconut

Family 2006